OPPORTUNITY SPOTTING

Creativity for corporate growth

Nigel MacLennan

Gower

Published by
Gower Publishing Limited
Gower House
Croft Road
Aldershot
Hampshire GU11 3HR

Gower
Old Post Road
Brookfield
Vermont 05036
USA

Nigel MacLennan has asserted his right under the Copyright, Designs and Patents Act 1988 to be identified as the author of this work.

British Library Cataloguing in Publication data

MacLennan, Nigel
  Opportunity Spotting: Creativity for
  Corporate Growth
  I. Title
  658

ISBN 0–566–07497–4

Library of Congress Cataloging-in-Publication Data
MacLennan, Nigel, 1961–
    Opportunity spotting: creativity for corporate growth / Nigel
  McLennan.
      p.   cm.
    Includes bibliographical references and index.
    ISBN 0–566–07497–4
    1. Creative ability in business. 2. Success in business.
  I. Title.
  HD53.M3   1994   94–9270
  650.1—dc20   CIP

Typeset in Palatino by Bournemouth Colour Graphics, Parkstone, Dorset and printed in Great Britain by Bookcraft Ltd, Midsomer Norton.

Contents

Preface

What can this book do for you?

Do you recognize this inevitable situation?

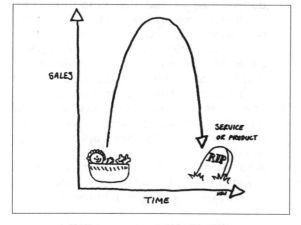

Product and sevice life cycle

You know you need to find opportunities, new products and services, before the inevitable happens, but . . .

You're not sure how to find them?

So you need something that will help you do this . . .

You have found it

The purpose of this book is to help you acquire the knowledge, learn the methods and develop the skills of Opportunity Spotting.

Opportunities must be actively sought. You can identify them by accident, but your chances of success are much greater if you take the process under your control rather than leaving it to fate. Bill Gates, now a multi-billionaire, avidly read all the available magazines and other information on the subject of computers in business.

This book will show you how to spot, seek and create opportunities that could lead to anything from mere survival to explosive growth and large profits.

The book will show you how:

- to be sensitive to spotting opportunities.
- to recognize opportunities.
- (and where) to seek opportunities.
- to create and build opportunities.
- to use empowering questions to generate opportunities.
- to make identified opportunities more usable.
- to identify the inevitable barriers to opportunities.
- to select and evaluate opportunities to follow.
- to choose the ideas that match your company.
- to develop and implement opportunity ideas.
- to overcome the obstacles and barriers.
- to create an opportunity culture.

Many organizations are becoming aware of the needs and benefits of helping their staff to be creative; it is a growing field. Like most emerging disciplines, there is a tendency towards, and probably an expectation of, gimmicky grammar, faddy phrases and other gibbering jargon. I have done my best to follow the norm (as just demonstrated). And I hope I've used unusual, amusing, and therefore easy to recognize and recall, names to describe the opportunity-spotting strategies.

A brief history of corporate creativity

There have been several books on the subject of commercial creativity. Other authors have started the process of making creative strategies understood by, and available to, the commercial world. Some have written in too academic a style to maintain the readers' interest. Others have given so much detail that they have obscured the principles. A few have smothered a relatively straightforward intellectual process in excessive jargon. One or two have tried to claim the discovery of divergent thinking (known for thousands of years) by attaching their own labels to the process. Still

more have advocated that a certain system (usually their own) must be followed if you are to be creative.

Corporate creativity has had a bad press – mainly caused by the above, but also because many previously offered methods failed. They failed for several reasons:

- Corporate creativity strategies were taught by people who had never run a business, and had certainly never used creative methods to establish one. Consequently the message had credibility as low as its source.
- There were few if any real-world examples of the strategies being successfully used (partly because of the previous point).
- The strategies were presented as the answer rather than as a guide or modifiable template.
- There was an excessive presentation of, dependence on, and alienation from, what I call psychological strategies. While they have their place and can be useful, psychological strategies are seen as 'attempts to create ideas out of thin air', methods that don't relate to the real commercial world with all its available information.
- There was little, if any in most cases, visual illustration to make the concepts memorable, entertaining, and rapidly understood.
- And worst of all, the critical nature of empowering questions as the control tool in creativity was largely ignored.

The objective of this book is: to rectify all the above failures; present a serious subject in a light-hearted and entertaining way, using cartoons in most instances; to give real-world examples of the strategies in operation; to present you with a series of exercises that will develop your thinking as you go along, to give you a creativity menu from which you can take idea snacks in abundance. Watch your wealth waistline!

Nigel MacLennan
1993

Anyone wishing to contact Nigel MacLennan may do so at:
1733 Coventry Road
South Yardley
Birmingham
B26 1DT

Acknowledgements

As with most major works of any kind, one name, or only a few names, will appear on the cover, when in fact a small army was required to produce it. The small army behind this work have my sincere thanks. My thanks to DJN, otherwise known as David Newton, for properly and professionally illustrating all my childlike cartoon sketches. My thanks to Sarah Allen for proof-reading the handouts on which this book is based, for pointing out the weaknesses in my writing, enabling me to improve. My thanks to my great friend Andrew Nicholson whose ruthlessly honest evaluations enabled me to get straight to the point. My thanks to a highly valued friend, formerly a member of my staff, Mary Mahon, for constantly reminding me of the need to practise with the same conviction that I preach. My thanks to Mark Griffiths for the encouragement given when the task seemed too big for me. To Gordon, formerly my brother, and now a great friend, for alerting me to many of the commercial events subsequently included in the book. The greatest thanks are due to my mother whose advice of yesteryear has improved over time to the point that I can now see her wisdom. My thanks also go to my mother for her willingness to forgo many of her opportunities to provide more for her children.

NM

Introduction

What are 'opportunities'? For the purposes of commercial survival, an opportunity needs to be a new or greatly improved product or service. Opportunities or innovations can happen in:

Small steps – where a series of continual and gradual improvements takes place. Most human advances are in small, often imperceptible steps.

Little jumps – where the status quo is changed by perceptible movement. Sony making micro tape recorder technology into a "Walkman' is an example.

Huge leaps – where an innovation is of such proportions that it changes an industry or even all of humanity. The Wright brothers' mastery of flight was one such leap.

The public perception of innovation is that it applies only to science and technology. But as you've probably gathered it is much, much wider than that. Innovation and Opportunity Spotting can be:

Technical	or	Scientific,
Process	or	Operational,
Structural	or	Organizational,
Marketing	or	Commercial,
Personal	or	Personnel in orientation.

An opportunity can be big or small, hugely profitable or a minor cost saving; it could be a grand innovation or a slight quality improvement; it could revolutionize an industry or make just one person's work more productive . . .

At this point you have a choice: you can skip the next few pages and go to the start of the Opportunity-Spotting strategies section if you wish. You probably know the needs for, and benefits of, innovation (or you wouldn't have bought this book!), and may not want to know the ingredients and workings of creativity. You don't need to understand creativity to use creative strategies any more than you need to know how an aeroplane works to be a commercial user of aviation.

You may, however, benefit enormously from reading the section about questions and their power on the pages immediately preceding Part I. If you are interested, the material on the next few pages may enable you to devise your own Opportunity-Spotting or commercial creativity strategies.

The need for and benefits of opportunity spotting

This section will tell you about the needs and benefits of Opportunity Spotting: why you should do it, what will happen if you don't, and what you can expect if you do.

Simply stated the reason for organized innovation and Opportunity Spotting is SURVIVAL.

Companies that choose not to 'Op-Spot' will ultimately perish. Some companies may put off that demise by chance. Some companies Op-Spot by complete accident. Others have it forced on them by customers. But companies that don't spot opportunities by some means will decline.

While the need for survival makes Opportunity Spotting an absolute requirement, there are several component needs and benefits.

Need: To counter product obsolescence

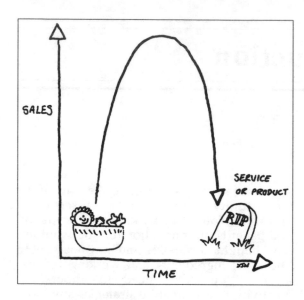

Product and service life cycle

All products and services have in-built obsolescence. (The only question is when?) Every product's life cycle is inherently limited. Today's 'whizz bang' product is tomorrow's artefact or curiosity, with a tiny specialist collector's market (at best!)

The benefit of Opportunity Spotting is survival and longevity.

Need: To counter stagnation

The risk in not engaging in Op-Spotting is corporate stagnation. Stagnating companies are usually forced to make just enough product or service change to barely survive. Such a 'skin of the teeth' policy appears to work when the world is stable and changes take place slowly. But it rarely is. Companies operating in such a way eventually go under at the hands of a last minute, desperate and too rapid change.

The benefit of Opportunity Spotting is potential growth.

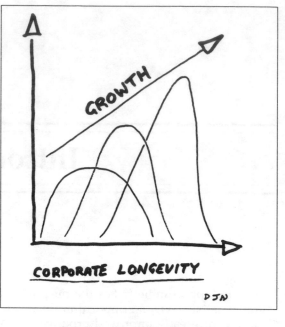

The benefits of Op-Spotting

Need: To counter 'one product vulnerability'

There is an especially strong need for Op-Spotting in 'one-product-wonder' companies. They are especially vulnerable to the inevitabilities of product obsolescence.

The benefits of Op-Spotting in this case cannot be overstated. The most successful companies have a systematic approach to product succession or R&D or ... . They may not call it Opportunity Spotting. In many companies no formal name exists for what they do, but do it they do. And they do it well.

Initiating and having an ongoing programme of Op-Spotting will increase (from one) the range and type of profitable products or services.

The benefit of Op-Spotting is that it can create a greater degree of stability through diversity.

Need: To counter chance factors

Since so many new products/services fail, you can't be sure to find 'the big one(s)' – the successor(s) to your current line – unless you systematically seek and create many 'Ops'. Approximately only 1 in 20 identified Ops will succeed. A large pipeline of Ops must be kept flowing to ensure adequate choice in product

2

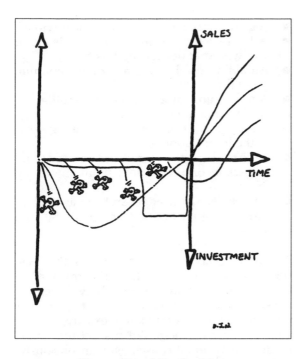

The reality of Op-Spotting

make proactive opportunity-seeking the norm.

Need: To counter strategic myopia

succession. Systematizing Opportunity Spotting minimizes the gambling element.

Another benefit: Systematic Op-Spotting maximizes the likelihood of success.

Need: To counter the 'reactive norm' of thinking

There is a need for Opportunity Spotting to be a formal process. Most executives are trained to solve problems as they arise (the reactive norm). They are trained towards, and selected for, risk-aversive behaviour. They are expected not to be dependent on creative forces.

The process of spotting opportunities is highly proactive. Successful entrepreneurs and intrapreneurs go out and actively look for information. They set up systems that enable them to access and interpret information.

If Op-Spotting can be made formal and encouraged as acceptable, even expected, behaviour, executives will feel the need to develop the necessary new skills. They will be motivated to adopt the new ways of thinking. Without an expectant and supportive attitude from management, team Opportunity Spotting will be weak, or reactive, at best.

Benefit: A formal op-spotting structure will

The most successful companies seem to consist of individuals with a shared cultural understanding of what the purpose of the company is. The recent fad for mission statements was used to try to bring that sense of unity and vision to less successful companies. For a company-wide sense of strategy, vision and purpose to exist, its constituent members must think, feel, and act towards the same goal. A mission statement covers the 'thinking' part. Oppotunity Spotting as a permanent company strategy covers all three parts. If everybody in the company is involved in Op-Spotting, if everybody knows that coming up with a suitable idea will be handsomely and proportionately rewarded, if everybody in the company knows that the very survival of their job depends on them spotting an opportunity, you will have collective, strategic 20/20 vision.

Benefit: Formal Op-Spotting gives strategy, vision and purpose, company-wide.

If you follow the material and complete the exercises in this book, you will do more than change a small aspect of your managerial behaviour; you could improve, immeasurably, your company's future. By the end of the book you will be in a position to make your company innovative and entrepreneurial. If you act on the information conveyed, you will reap the rewards of structured opportunity seeking.

You could become the spearhead of your company's dynamic growth.

In addition, the book is designed to be used either as a training and development tool or as a creativity methods menu – or for less hygienic uses if you are not entirely satisfied with the product.

Exercise: Which of the needs listed above are the most pressing needs for Opportunity Spotting in your company? What other needs can you envisage?

Exercise: What other benefits are there to be gained from Opportunity Spotting? Which benefits are most relevant to your company?

The characteristics and ingredients of opportunity spotting

Opportunity focus v. Problem focus

Opportunity Spotting is distinct from, but can involve, problem solving. Opportunity detection does not need a problem to focus your attention (although that is a legitimate strategy). Nothing is problematic about an artist's canvas before the work starts. Nothing was 'wrong' with board games before *Monopoly* was invented. To spot opportunities you do not need problems. But problems can alert you to the benefits of finding an opportunity.

Information dependent and independent

Successful Opportunity Spotting can be conducted independently without any reference to problems or information. But if it is undertaken with the use of information it can be enormously effective. As will be seen later there are strategies available for circumstances in which information is available and not available.

Other ingredients

In terms of other ingredients, Opportunity Spotting is very similar to successful creativity. Both require several components to be present at the same time.

There must be:

- A goal/a target (conscious or unconscious).
- A high level of desire (you have desire or you wouldn't be reading this book).
- An ability level above a certain minimum (low) threshold.
- A method of gathering the information.
- An information base to draw on.
- A structure for processing or making sense of the information.
- Time to shape the ingredients in your mind (conscious or unconscious brain processing time).
- The skills, knowledge and persistence to turn the opportunity from potential into actual.

The *unconscious brain* ingredient is the least understood. We know that the mysterious unconscious is involved in creativity somehow, we know many methods that seem to prompt it into action, but we don't know exactly, or even vaguely, how it works. We suspect that information can be input consciously, unconsciously, or both, and that information can be processed consciously, unconsciously or both. In short we know the ingredients, but we don't know how they come together to bake the creativity cake.

In relation to the ingredients of Opportunity Spotting the objectives of this book are:

1 To provide you with various methods of gathering opportunity information.

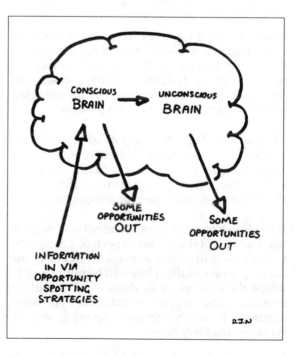

Product and service life cycle

2 To provide structures and systems for processing that information.

3 To provide you with psychological strategies to prompt the unconscious mind.

4 To provide you with a sufficient understanding of Opportunity-Spotting strategies to be able to create your own.

Creating your own strategies

Knowledge is power and ignorance is bliss

Creativity seems to be related to extremes of all sorts: madness and genius, saturated knowledge and complete ignorance, systematic method and casual spontaneity, shocking deviance and nauseating conformity . . . Enough said.

Most of the factors seem beyond control, but you can (?) create your creativity creations with the following creativity components.

Altering the focus of your thought

Seek to alter the foreground or background of your intellectual landscape. In other words if you are looking for an opportunity in, say, a company department you could direct your thinking towards the department (foreground) or the context in which the department operates in the company (background). You can also choose to focus on the interaction between foreground and background.

Altering the type of thinking used

- PACS: Perception Altering Creativity Strategies.
- PECS: Process Editing Creativity Strategies.

Being creative requires an alteration in the way you think or in what you think. To change the way you think about something, anything, you can alter your *Perceptions* or your way of *processing*. The difference between the two can be seen in the contrast between 'I'll believe it when I see it/ and 'I'll see it when I believe it', – or in our terms: 'I'll start processing like that when I've perceived the evidence' and 'I'll perceive the evidence when I've started processing like that'. Although they can be thought of as separate, processing and perception are inseparably linked. What you think affects how you think and vice versa. Most creativity methods lean towards one or the other, for the sake of simplicity. When devising strategies I suggest you do too.

Go give those PACS and PECS a work out.

Using thought tools

Having chosen the foreground or background and decided whether to affect processing or perception, you need an intellectual tool to complete your new Opportunity-Spotting strategy.

One of the main purposes of this book is to provide you with a range of creative thought strategies. Many are based on a few simple tools, for example challenging (the rules), modifying (the boundaries), widening, narrowing . . . Indeed, too many to mention. More probably, there are more than you can mention . . . and probably a few more again! Since the book is so full of examples of creativity strategies, there is little point in providing any here.

Exercise: After having read the book, and seen many examples, return to this section, jog your memory, and devise a few Opportunity-Spotting strategies of your own.

The Opportunity-Spotting 10 step process requirements

Before you can stand alongside a successfully implemented opportunity, there are ten steps that need to be taken:

1 Accept the need. You and/or others will have to accept and acknowledge the need to seek, spot or create opportunities.

2 Acquire the methods. You will have to acquire at least some methods, techniques or strategies to generate opportunities.

3 Be in an 'opportunity-positive culture'. Lone entrepreneurs find this stage easy; all they have to do is control their own thoughts. If you are dependent on the views, support and assistance of others you may need to create an opportunity-positive culture before opportunity seeking. Or if you have come up with an idea, you may have to 'culture create' before trying to implement it.

4 Start spotting, seeking and creating opportunities. Use the methods you have acquired here or devised yourself.

5 Enhance the ideas you generate. Put some meat on the skeleton, make the idea more practical and orientated toward the real world.

6 Evaluate and choose those you wish to take to the next stage.

7 Develop and implement the ideas.

8 Overcome the barriers. There are bound to be several, some of which will be self-imposed.

9 Build or fill an opportunity pipeline. Not every idea you generate will work. To make sure you have enough ideas for product succession, there is a requirement to have a pipeline of ideas in development.

10 Conventional management takes over. When an idea comes to fruition, normal management methods take over.

Each of the points above will be expanded elsewhere, but now let us examine the use of, and the difference between, spotting, seeking and creating strategies.

Using the Opportunity-Spotting methods

Any one method can be used to spot, seek or create opportunities.

Spotting

Having acquired a knowledge of the various strategies, you will be able to spot opportunities by recognising the right commercial ingredients when you see them in your environment.

Seeking

Rather than depending on passive recognition you can choose to actively seek opportunities Use the source methods to determine what raw data to gather and the kind of information to extract from it.

Creating

Creating opportunities requires you to go further than when spotting or seeking. You need to look for situations in which some opportunity ingredient is missing from a known recipe. The task is to find ways in which you can complete the recipe to cook an opportunity.

Many analytical people will underestimate or even ignore the relatively passive, chance-dependent spotting strategies in favour of more controlled, information-dependent seeking and creation strategies. That is an error: information-rich is not know-how wealthy. Many innovations occur by accident, as a result of observing the effects of something that happened unexpectedly while exercising know-how or practising a craft such as medicine. In *The Alarming History Of Medicine* Richard Gordon convincingly argues that most medical advances have been by accident.

However since analysis is the main tool of business, it makes sense to favour the more information-dependent strategies. There is the added assurance that the more passive strategies may work by default; if the analytical strategies don't produce anything themselves they may lead to an opportunity being discovered by accident.

Overlap of methods

As you read through or pick and choose from the various strategies, you may notice that some of them either overlap or are similar to each other. The overlap is intentional. Neither you nor I would want to miss an opportunity by not recognizing its ingredients because we saw them from an unfamiliar perspective.

The importance of questions

There is one strategy that is common to all other Op-Spotting methods and that is the asking of questions.

All the Op-Spot methods presented are, and can only be, pointers to which questions to ask, guides to what type of questions to ask and how to ask them. The Op-Spot methods will give pointers to which directions will be useful to follow.

Your ability to ask constructive and empowering questions, once on the right route, will determine the destination at which you will arrive.

Ask positive questions and get positive results; ask negative questions and get negative results. If I asked you to give five reasons why you were destined for success, your mind would search itself and find five reasons. If you had been asked similarly to explain why you would be a failure, your mind would have sifted through its massive storehouse and given you what was asked of it.

A positive, expectant mind asks positive, empowering, expectant questions which produce positive, empowering and results-orientated answers. The aphorism 'Be careful what you ask for, you may get it' is more prophetic in real life than any crystal ball has ever been in fiction. The answer you get to your question is determined by the way you ask it. Phrase your opportunity-searching questions in such a way that the only option is a positive empowering answer.

Positive empowering questions should be:

- Open not closed: That is, they can't sensibly be answered with a Yes or No. 'Is it daytime?' is a closed question. 'What is daytime?' is an open question.
- Specifically directed: That is, aimed directly at yourself or others, as opposed to being a vague 'at no one in particular' question.
- Ability assuming/empowering: The questions must contain an implicit or explicit assumption of available ability or power.
- Positively expectant: The questions must be asked in such a way that a positive answer is the only acceptable option available to your mind.

As you go through the book you'll see plenty of examples to help you get into the habit of asking positive empowering questions. Examples of empowering questions that were asked by successful innovators and Opportunity Spotters are given. Examples of appropriate questions are given with each method.

Means of presentation

To examine the individual methods in detail, the format throughout, with rare exceptions, will be:

1 Title of the opportunity source or method.
2 Principle behind the method.
3 Example(s) of the method's use.
4 Examples of 'how to use it' empowering questions.
5 Relevant exercises to take your thinking further.
6 Illustrative cartoon.

Now let's look at the methods you can use to generate, and places you can find information on, potential opportunities.

PART I

Generating opportunities

1

External Sources

An external source of opportunity is defined as some place, event, observation that exists/occurs outside the company or organization in which you are working. In other words the information that you convert into an opportunity comes from anywhere other than inside your organization. An internal source of opportunity is obtained from using information available inside your company.

There are three sub-categories or sub-sources of external opportunities:

- Outside-observation-led opportunities
- Problem-led opportunities
- Solution-led opportunities

Outside observation sources

- Unexpected outside event
- Industry/market structure changes
- Demographics
- Political pointers
- Enticing environmental enterprise
- Changes in perception
- Significant point
- Variable value
- Trends
- Fads
- Symbolism
- Convention bucking
- Hypocrisy opportunities
- Market analysis
- Challenge I
- Challenge II
- Niches
  - Toll-gate
  - Speciality skill
  - Speciality market
  - Location strategy
- Calendar opportunities

Unexpected outside event

A surprise scenario occurs. Something completely unexpected should alert you to the possibility of there being an opportunity. For example astronomers have long cursed interstellar dust for obscuring their view of the heavens. While Harold Kroto was trying to

Unexpected outside event

understand the composition of the dust, his analysis threw up an unexpected phenomenon – namely the presence of a substance that did not exist. Others had dismissed the findings as a glitch but Kroto suggested they represented the presence of carbon-60. He was right. The characteristics of this newly discovered form of carbon make its potential simply breathtaking.

A second example: the history of IBM in the personal computers field shows that the apparent inexplicability of people being interested in the early PCs was what alerted them to the opportunity. "'It couldn't happen' is what made us pay attention to the event. They were too expensive and had so little capability no one would want them."

Wrong! Kids started playing computer games, parents saw the office potential and wanted a machine. There lay the birth of an unexpected market.

How can you use this method? Simply by asking the following kinds of questions:

- What has happened recently that raised my eyebrows?
- What unexpected event has happened in the world, national or local news?
- What is there in trade journals or other written sources?
- What has startled me about other companies?
- When ... Who ... How ... Why ... Where ... ?

IMPORTANT EXERCISE: After each Op-Source method, devise at least two questions of the above type. One should be relevant to your company. It is vital that you carry out this exercise. As stated before the most important tool in corporate creativity is the asking of empowering questions. Like any newly acquired skill, it takes practice to get into the habit of effortless competence.

Industry/market structure changes

The realization of an opportunity always causes market or structure changes. And more opportunities are always present when these changes occur. There are four pointers to opportunities, or four clues to imminent or further change:

- Rapid growth.
- Inappropriate market segmentation.

- Convergence of technologies.
- Change in method.

Rapid growth

In many (most?) industries and businesses, where existing practices remain unchanged because they work, they inevitably become obsolete. Time always renders yesterday's best possible system second-rate and relatively

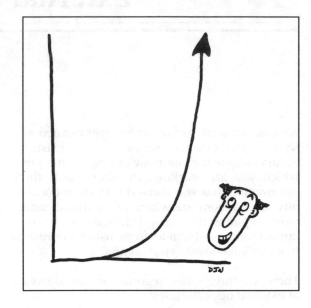

Rapid growth

inefficient. In such a situation the emergence of competitors, or more likely, newcomers is probable. They see the obsolescence, come in dramatically and take huge market shares. The new efficient systems these competitors bring often marks the beginning of a period of rapid growth, (for example Telecoms, PCs ...).

Identifying obsolete systems or operating methods in other industries is one way in which this method will road-sign an opportunity. Which industries have been unchanged for a long time? Which businesses have *a* way and an *only* way of doing things? You can identify and capitalize on a rapid growth by watching which companies are expanding fast and finding a way of getting 'in on the action'.

Inappropriate market segmentation

Look for low-profile parts of a market that are ignored by others. In the radio broadcasting industry of the 1950s and 1960s it was thought that housewives at home with their pre-school children or doing housework after the children

12

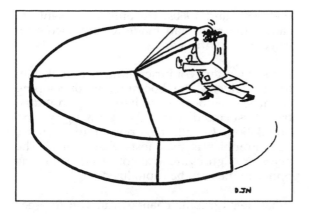

Inappropriate market segmentation

Convergence of technologies

had gone to school were the main daytime radio audience. Advertising on radio was thus aimed at that market – inappropriately as it turned out. The largest segment is actually people at work or driving around in connection with their work. The first broadcasters to act on this information obtained much better advertising results for their clients and increased their share of the listening market, thereby commanding higher advertising fees.

Identify the 'low return' segments which have been marginalized by those operating a 'creaming' policy. What awkward new requests for service are dismissed as not fitting in with the range on offer? What recent or current changes have been perceived as 'fads' where in fact emerging market changes are occurring? Where an industry segments a market in such a way that a customer or potential customer group has been ignored or marginalized, you have an opportunity. Finding a way to satisfy these people could be the start of a major market structure change.

Convergence of technologies

Bringing together two or more previously separate technologies can create huge opportunities and market structure changes. Wang brought typewriting and computers together to make the word processor. Result: both markets changed, one negatively and the other with positively explosive growth.

There are possibly hundreds of new industries waiting to be created by bringing together previously separate technologies.

What five technologies or gadgets do you know most about? Choose two of them, not necessarily high-tech (the windsurfer isn't, see

later under Transfer), and put them together conceptually; what could that create? How could you combine them to do something, anything? Try different ways of connecting them. Try different gadgets. Try combining three, four, five of them. Try altering their permutations or combinations. All the time ask yourself empowering questions.

Change in method

When the mass-production of cars was introduced, Ford and eventually others capitalized on the change in manufacturing method. Rolls-Royce capitalized too, but in a different way. Their view was that mass-produced cars had become common. While everyone else had seen the changes in method as rendering the old methods obsolete, Rolls-Royce saw it as an opportunity to sell cars of distinction: hand-made cars of superior quality, made the way cars 'should' be made, and sold to – and only to – those of sufficiently high standing to appreciate the value of the product. The rest is history.

Telephone technology has been around since the nineteenth century. Digitalization of pictures has been known of for more than 40 years; copying technology has been around for decades. When the three were brought together the resultant fax revolutionized business

Change in method

communication. A whole new industry emerged almost overnight, and fortunes were made by some very ordinary people.

Keep a log of the changes in method you come across. Go further: actively seek out changes in method. Then ask yourself questions like: How can I use this method to ... ? In what ways can I improve ... using this method?

Demographics

There is profit in watching people and population changes, changes in such factors as birth rate, family size, mortality rates, quality of health, longevity (pre- and post-retirement), educational levels, location and people mobility, labour force composition, wealth-spread patterns, typical consumption cycles from birth to death of individuals, segmentation within these variables/markets, and many, many other demographic variables.

Trammell Crow, a Dallas real-estate developer, foresaw the accommodation (demographic) opportunities contained in the baby boom of

Demographics

the 1950s and 1960s. He built apartments to satisfy the need and made a very successful career (to say the least).

In most western countries, industries that cater for the elderly are booming. In developing countries, the booms are happening in industries associated with the growing young population. Of all the opportunity sources, demographics is the most reliable of all. The necessary figures are available years before the opportunities can be capitalized on.

What demographic changes can you foresee? Which businesses will be affected by these? Which will prosper? Which will suffer? How can you profit from the sufferers or beneficiaries? What knock-on effects will these changes have? How can you ...? When will ...?

Political pointers to profit

Changes brought about by politicians, or proposals for change, can open opportunities for the astute current affairs follower. Lenin (of the Russian Revolution – the first one) publicly stated that all his country's people should learn to read and write. An aware businessman, Armand Hammer, realized that the newly re-created Russian state had no writing implements. He approached Lenin to obtain a manufacturing concession (free enterprise needed special concessions) to make the pencils required to achieve Lenin's goals. Hammer was by default granted a virtual national monopoly. There started an enormously successful business career.

In the UK, education policy was changed in the late 1980s to encourage schools to manage themselves. Many companies were either set up, or directed themselves, to exploit the change. They offered computer software to assist in managing schools, training in the relevant business management skills to appropriate staff ...

If you do keep in touch with current affairs, this is a strategy for which all the information is easily obtainable. In fact you are given the ingredients of your opportunity free, or nearly free on radio, television, in the press and so on. If you don't follow current affairs I would not suggest you start doing so just to use this strategy; there are plenty of others available to you.

What is the significant political change of the moment, and where in that could you best look for opportunities? What needs to be provided to make these policies happen?

EXERCISE: List five major policy shifts in the last few years. For each one, identify two opportunities that were, or could have been, exploited by you.

Enticing environmental enterprise

With the growing demand to preserve and enhance the environment for our children, grandchildren and all future generations comes many opportunities. They occur in, and can be identified from, at least six overlapping areas.

Specialist waste disposal

Many waste products can't be dumped in the usual domestic fashion; they are too toxic. There have long been industrial waste disposal companies. As we are becoming a chemically more sophisticated society there will be an ongoing chain of opportunities for individuals and companies who devise ingenious ways of

containing and disposing of specialist waste products – not just chemical.

Waste processing

Much waste is disposed of when in fact with a little thought it could probably be recycled or used in another way (see Variable value). There are several companies who will provide microbes and bacteria that will convert various waste products into useful substances. Find out what those microbes are. If this is an opportunity you could capitalize on, it would be smart to collate a list of these useful conversion bacteria, a list of their applications, and to seek out new ways of using them, possibly by conducting intellectual experiments in the first instance.

Waste recycling

There is already a large industry recycling paper, plastic, glass, metal . . . There is however one obvious mis-match opportunity (see Mis-matches) available to anyone who chooses to take it up. The people who provide the raw material to this industry receive little, or no, payment for their efforts or resources. Increasingly people will see there is money in their garbage can. The person or organization that devises a method which allows individuals to obtain, directly, a return for their waste will have a splendid opportunity. What could that be? A smokeless waste-burning unit to generate heat? A fertilizer creation unit from human waste? Find at least two ways to get a return from each of the following: faeces, paper, waste water, metal, glass, plastic, waste heat (excess heat from sources like weather, dirty hot water, cooking heat . . .). If you can't see two opportunities in each, what could you do to find them?

Self-contained energy generation systems

The person or company that can invent a commercially viable self-contained energy generation system will have an opportunity of unprecedented proportions. By self-contained I mean that the fuel is self-generating/creating and using its own waste products; it will also provide self-cooling for the energy conversion process.

Far-fetched? Not a bit of it! Algae when dried and ground are as flammable as powdered coal. The algae are self-re-creating. They consume carbon dioxide to grow and multiply. The carbon dioxide and water which are generated from the engine as waste products provide the living environment for the algae. They require water and heat to thrive: that heat can be provided by heat transfer from the engine's liquid cooling system. The heat and energy to dry and grind the algae is also provided by the engine. Still think it's far-fetched? Well, there is a working prototype in existence and it is being improved.

What is the attraction, in terms of environmental needs, of this engine? How can you invent a similar unit?

Greenhouse effect/ozone depletion counteraction methods

The 'alleged' effect (it is not conclusively proven) that CFCs are having on the environment (depletion of the ozone layer) has forced the manufacture of other non-CFC foam materials, refrigerants and so on. As you might imagine, the manufacturers of these 'friendlier' materials have an enormous opportunity both for high sales and high levels of favourable publicity. The known carcinogenic effects on our skin of a depleted ozone layer is dramatically increasing the sales of sun tan lotions which are now being increasingly perceived as skin protection creams. Indeed a new entry to the market has been the emergence of total sun block creams. Which countries do you think will enable you to benefit most from this kind of opportunity?

Our current global warming hypothesis is that increased CO_2 levels in the environment traps heat radiation in the atmosphere and thereby increases the ambient temperature. That sce-

nario is perceived by the doomsayers to be a threat, but on the flip side of any threat there is opportunity. What opportunities will global warming provide for you?

Assume that the hypothesis is correct and that it is harmful. If CO_2 levels are rising, what is the obvious opportunity? It is to look for a means that can reduce CO_2 levels and make it commercially viable. What phenomena do we know of that reduce CO_2? Trees 'eat' CO_2, plankton (microscopic 'sea algae') eat CO_2. How can you capitalize on plankton eating CO_2? Possibly by identifying the most CO_2-efficient, or fastest breeding plankton, or by genetically engineering a specially resistant strain that could function in polluted waters, or . . . Find five opportunities for using plankton, and identify five groups of people who might buy your idea.

Nature's coercion

Nature 'fights back' occasionally and makes human life so intolerable that we have to do something about the problem. The pea-soupers (thick, pollution-laden fog) in London (1950s) and other cities caused by industrial and domestic smoke pollution forced our genetic predecessors into action: the Clean Air Act was passed. What opportunities do you think that created? What kinds of supplies and services do you think were in demand?

Other cities, even today, are infamous for their smog. There are opportunities for items like pollution masks, household air filter systems,

catalytic convertors . . . This is likely to be an increasing source of opportunity when medical trends like the quadrupling of the numbers of asthma sufferers in recent years become more publicly known.

Would you believe that in The Netherlands pig manure now has to be buried underground, because ammonia fumes coming off the pig waste create toxic rain which falls across the country? Somebody somewhere will be making money from that. What do you think would be required to exploit this opportunity?

Regulation enforcement opportunities

Environmental or public health departments are charged with enforcing most public hygiene and safety regulations. Every time a new regulation appears a whole range of new services to help companies and individuals comply seem to pop up overnight.

Keep a note of new regulations as they are announced, and at a later date look for ways in which they contain opportunities for your company.

Changes in perception

Most aspects of life can be seen from many different viewpoints. Frequently whole industries are changed very rapidly because of the way the mass of people change their view on something, recent changes in health perception for example. The perception change which led to the desirability of obtaining and maintaining health could not have been predicted. But when it arrived, many companies, capitalized on it, for example health magazines, nutritional supplement companies, health food stores . . . People started to see their health as being more controllable.

More importantly, from a business perspective, they started to see health as something worth investing in – an asset worth enhancing and protecting. They started to realize that prevention is cheaper and more enjoyable than the cure. So they felt they had to buy the products and services that aimed at achieving that control. Aerobics classes were established and once the market established itself there was an evolution into Step Aerobics; no doubt there will be future evolutions. What will they be? How can you engineer an evolution in this market?

What changes in perception can you see? Go through the main industry sectors: what can you see? Who might be in a better position to see perception changes? Can you identify any changes which might happen with a little (marketing) help? Changes in perception are often prompted by trendsetters (for example Bob Geldof). So what are today's trendsetters saying?

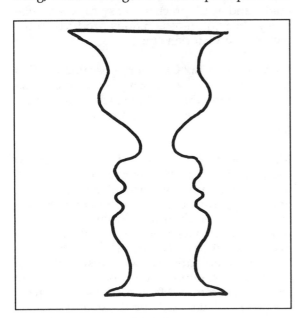

Changes in perception

Significant point

Significant point

In any outside event there is always a single, key or significant point. For UK exporters the significant point about the 1992 devaluation (by default) of sterling was that it made exporting more competitive. Most popular products or services sell because of one significant point/benefit. The significant point about the Reject Shop is that customers are willing to buy slightly imperfect goods because the fault doesn't matter, but the reduced price does.

The significant point identified will depend upon your perspective and your background context. If you can't see an opportunity from your own perspective, imagine yourself in someone else's shoes.

What is the most significant point in the news today? . . . the company report? . . . any idea that comes up?

Variable value

The value of anything varies over time, over location, over use and over ownership.

A standard car bought in the early part of this century had no special value, but now (over time) in the same condition its value is enormous. A chainsaw has little value in the West, but in several developing countries, it is worth up to ten times its western value because it provides a living, cutting trees, for the owner (over location).

A copy of this book has an enormous potential value to you, but may only be slightly more pleasing than a brick for someone wishing (over use) to prop up an uneven table! A house with a small plot of land may be a tax liability to one person, but to the person who owns all the surrounding land and can't develop it until s/he acquires the remaining piece of the jigsaw, the land is worth just a little more (over ownership) to say the least.

To find opportunity in variable value, devise and ask yourself the following kinds of questions: To whom could this be more valuable? Where could this/these be more valuable? When could this be more valuable? Could its value change over time, location, use or ownership? Who would pay you to take away the metaphorical horse dung because they don't want it *and* who would pay you to supply horse dung because they do want it?

Variable value

Trends/trendy top up

A trend can be towards something, or away from something. Or more likely, both towards one thing and away from something else simultaneously. Laura Ashley capitalized on the vacuum left behind in a trend towards high fashion. In the 1950s when life was being increasingly dictated by fashion, Laura Ashley made and sold practical, easy-to-wear, relatively cheap, non-ostentatious products in the style of the Victorian era.

More recently Liz Claibourne became the first to recognize and establish a successful business satisfying the trend towards stylish, practical women's business attire which is not faddish.

Many trends have evolved and developed recently. Use of PCs, increased air travel, increase in leisure pursuits and leisure time . . . Some are permanent shifts in the market; others are fads or short-term fashions and may require more investment to get into than can ever be obtained as a return. The trick here is to spot the trend early enough, be sure it is not just a fad and figure out a way your company can benefit from it. Many manufacturers have dismissed what they thought would be a fad to their cost. When Sony introduced the Sony Walkman it was largely ignored by competitors, until it was too late. The Sony Walkman became the recognized name for a personal stereo just as the Hoover was/is the name people use for a vacuum cleaner.

A similar commercial victory was obtained by the new manufacturers of mountain bikes. The established bike manufacturers dismissed mountain bikes as a fad, and now a whole new range of names dominates the bike industry.

What trends are taking place right now? In which areas would your company be best suited to look for trends? Where can you find out about trends? What vacuum is being left behind in a trend towards something? How could you fill that vacuum? What are the trends relevant to your industry? Your company? Your department?

Fads

Many fads (short-lived crazes or preferences for largely useless and impractical items) will cost you more to get into than you can ever hope to get back in return. However for the flexible manufacturer, the emergence or indeed creation of a fad can prove to be extremely profitable. There are many examples: hula hoops, pogo sticks, Space Hoppers, skateboards, Frisbees, Cabbage Patch Dolls, Bogglins, platform shoes, Rubik's cubes, water beds, digital watches, pocket calculators (even for people who didn't need them). Be alert

though: many apparent fads have turned out to be long-term product lines, such as skateboards.

How can you recognize an emerging fad? It will probably be something inherently useless, but which in some way provides entertainment (even if only for a very short while, until the novelty has worn off). It may symbolize some attitude or mood. The mood most often caught by fads is childish abandon, childish excitement or interest. Frequently some product or other may do well because it addresses a serious need and has a fad element to it – like digital watches.

What has captured the childish side of your personality recently? What has intrigued you for its own sake, but which has no serious use? If you have children, or friends with children, what kinds of things are they excited by now? If you come up with an idea, try it out on the kids.

Symbolism

This strategy is a close relative of Fads and Trends. The opportunity is realized if you can find something that symbolically captures the current cultural mood, if you can find a product that expresses, or can be linked to, the prevalent feeling of the time.

Mary Quant detected the mood and satisfied it in the 1960s with her miniskirt design. She pro-

Hypocrisy opportunities

vided symbolic expression of Swinging London with her cheap mass-produced clothes. Symbolism is the strategy most likely to be used by the fashion industry. But it can be enjoyed elsewhere. Any product or service in any industry that can symbolically express the cultural mood of the time will be more sought after than one that doesn't.

What is the mood of today? How can you find out what it is? What other symbols can you copy or mimic and apply them to your product or service? Symbolism could be used in conjunction with Designer derivatives.

Convention bucking

Convention bucking is an intimate partner to each of the previous three strategies. People like to rebel against all sorts of things: their parents, authority, traditions . . . In the 1920s Coco Chanel gave women the means to rebel against Victorian prudishness by introducing and marketing 'loud' make-up (or at least that is how it was seen at the time). Make-up became the product vehicle for bucking Victorian conventions.

Before you can buck a convention you need to identify it. What conventions would you like to buck? What do you feel oppressed by? What product vehicle would allow you to buck a convention off your back? What conventions do you impose? You can be sure one of your staff, at least, would like to buck them. How can you encourage the constructive use of convention bucking in your work place?

An intimate, but not so open, partner to the previous four strategies. We are all hypocrites. Would the hypocrite who wishes to deny it, please stand. We usually tolerate our own and the hypocrisy of others. When a hypocrite goes too far we are reminded that hypocrisy exists. Occasionally the sense of 'hypocrisy gone too far' can spark an opportunity. In the 1930s, 40s, 50s (and . . . well, best not say too recently; they might still be alive, and in litigious mood!), movie tycoons were widely thought to be more inclined (reclined?) to use the casting couch as a selector of actresses (and actors?) than relevant factors such as acting ability. Everyone in the industry knew that, but on screen love-

making was never shown and was only rarely hinted at. There was a widespread sense of hypocrisy.

Hugh Heffner noted and chose to act on this observation. He made a fortune by setting up and publishing *Playboy*.

Where have you noticed barefaced hypocrisy recently? Go through a list of social groups and try to tag at least one incidence of hypocrisy on each. Which of these strike you as the most obvious and shameful? In what five ways could you exploit that hypocrisy?

Market analysis strategies

Many companies pay lip-service to market research and the other conventional market analysis methods. So while these strategies are more like conventional management tools than other Opportunity-Spotting strategies, they can provide ideas if used properly, as illustrated in the examples. There are five market analysis opportunities.

- Market size
- Competitive analysis
- Existing market research
- New market research (concerns collections)
- Speciality marketing.

Market size

Market sizes can change very quickly for unpredicatable reasons. Conduct a regular examination of market size. Many opportunities can be obtained by keeping a close eye on what is happening in the market-place for your products/services. Sainsbury's (the UK supermarket chain) now conduct regular reviews of the market. They study size, what is bought, where it is bought . . .

Unexpected new customers can appear in a market overnight. In the VCR market, people have always had difficulty operating the machines, but have been too ashamed to admit it. A few people (a small market) sought simple machines. Now people have 'come out' and openly seek idiot-proof machines. The size of this market is increasing and the British company Amstrad are targeting it directly.

Conduct a regular examination of your markets. What size is the market? Is it growing? Shrinking? In what ways are the segments altering? Who is coming into the market for the first time? Who is leaving it and why? What are they buying instead? Conduct a regular SWOT analysis. List five ways you could capitalize on each of the changes you have observed. The acid test of your market understanding is: can you genuinely answer all reasonable and relevant questions about your market by an intelligent, but uninformed business person? This strategy is related and similar to the Needs analysis and Industry/market structure changes strategies and may be most powerfully used in conjunction with them.

Competitive analysis

As in war, often the winning strategy in business is based on exploiting the weakness of the enemy. Conducting a detailed competitor analysis will undoubtedly generate many opportunity ideas. Competitive analysis is a highly detailed opportunity strategy and will suit best the analytical personality. Since there are many books on the subject no attempt will be made to cover the methods here. The reader is referred to *Corporate Strategy* by I. Ansoff, 1965 or the 1987 revised edition published by Penguin; and *Competitive Strategy* by M. Porter, 1980, Free Press.

Existing market research

Gathering information from your existing customers can give you extremely accurate market research information. It will also demonstrate to your customers that you are serious about those ubiquitous claims to superiority.

Johnson Controls (Milwaukee, USA) makes climatic control systems. Historically it has competed against its larger rivals (for example, Honeywell) on the basis of price. Johnson management conducted a market research analysis with their customers. It emerged, much to the Johnson team's surprise, that customers were not so interested in initial price as they were in the total cost of installation and maintenance, and particularly in convenience and rapidity of maintenance and installation. Johnson devised and marketed a new system (Metasys) based on ease of installation, ease of maintenance and low cost. First-year sales were $500 million. Need I say more about this strategy?

New market research

The expressed concerns and irritations of today are the markets of tomorrow. Robert Taylor at the Minnetonka Corporation has his team scan hundreds of scientific and other journals each month to see what concerns consumers and others. Since Taylor has been responsible for several fads and innovations we can assume the strategy works.

What sources of customer concerns could you be accessing? Where can you observe customers demonstrably expressing their needs?

Speciality marketing

Strongly related to Symbolism, this strategy highlights the opportunities contained in people buying products or services as much for their intrinsic use as for the wish to be identified with the marketing method or image. To use this strategy you should create a unique marketing proposition (UMP) in the same way that you identify or create a unique selling proposition (USP) for your product. If appropriate, your marketing should make some sort of image or philosophical statement.

The Italian clothes manufacturer, Benetton, are probably more identified with their controversial marketing statements than with their products. They have a UMP.

What UMP or image do your customers want to be associated with? Or to be more specific, what compromise image would express all or most of your customer segments?

Challenge 1

Adopt the 'You old fool' mentality. The young seem to do this naturally, particularly around

adolescence. Many of them criticize the *status quo* and challenge what seems OK to their elders. An initial unwillingness to accept things the way they are appears to be essential for making progress. If Edison hadn't challenged the 'gas lighting is OK' school of thought it might have been many years before someone else invented the electric light. Don't accept that because something '*is;*' it is OK.

Challenge I

Criticize the *status quo*. Choose an aspect of the way an industry or market works and find fault with it. If you were setting up such a market/industry/product . . . now, how would you do it? Challenge what seems OK. If it seems OK, it's probably a long time since anyone has sought ways to improve it. Nothing should be exempt from challenge – least of all that which seems above reproach. Critically assess all the assumptions on which any procedure/system/department/product . . . is based. What is wrong with those assumptions? In what ways has history made these assumptions obsolete? What could replace them?

Challenge 2   Invert the foundations

Identify the assumptions underpinning an industry, market or product. State the opposite of the original assumptions, then pull them together and build on them.

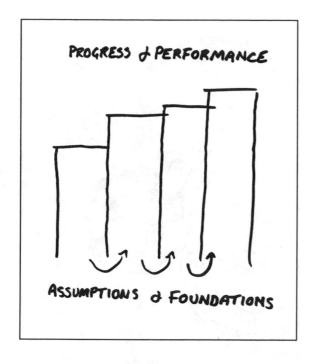

Challenge II

Toll-gate strategy

King C. Gillette built a huge business from thinking of the old-fashioned cut-throat razors: 'Why do they go to all the expense and trouble of fashioning a backing that has nothing to do with shaving?' It is debatable whether he challenged or inverted the assumptions implicitly in this question. But I believe he inverted them: the assumption was that the backing was required to support the edge; he asserted it was not required. History proved him right.

Although this strategy can be used in any context I suggest you identify a stable business or market, one in which, *de facto*, no new thinking has taken place for some time, and start identifying the assumptions and turning them on their heads.

Put yourself in a position where everyone who wants to buy a particular product *HAS* to buy your part of the overall package – even if that part is very small. Microsoft's DOS and Intel's processing chips make stunning examples.

Speciality skill

You become so specialized and so expert in the practice of your art, that you effectively carve out a niche for yourself. For example, in the automotive electricals industry a few names dominate the entire field with their speciality skill (Lucas, Bosch, Delco).

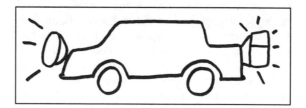

Speciality skill

Niches

There are several types of commercial niche positions, each of which presents opportunities. All niches consist of several overlapping elements, ingredients or components. The four that present the best opportunities are:

- Toll-gate strategy.
- Speciality skill.
- Speciality market.
- Location strategy.

Speciality market

To carve a niche in a speciality market, knowledge is your most important tool. Obtaining and maintaining superior market knowledge to your competitor's is the key. The Swiss owned SGS Ltd is a leading (the leader in UK) inspections and verifications company. Based

on people's distrust of each other, this industry theoretically requires the most up-to-date knowledge of all the regulations and measurement standards as applied to every market worldwide! Plus a constantly up-dated knowledge of who is in what market, and exactly what they need.

If any industry typifies the speciality market strategy, the inspections and verifications industry does. The willingness to acquire and develop whatever skills are necessary to respond to and exploit specialist market knowledge ahead of anyone else is the tactic required to turn this strategy into opportunity.

Location strategy

This is a combination of the previous three strategies as applied at a local level. Being the only bakery, cinema, garage in town fills the location niche. Many of the big chain-store companies use this strategy: for example, they try to be the only supermarket in a small town. Once in position, it is no longer viable for anyone to compete on that scale. The key here is to find a place where your product/service should be available but isn't at present. And if you made it available it would occupy a localized monopoly.

Do any of your products have a necessary role in any other process or product? Could any of them be altered in such a way as to fulfil the needs of a Toll-gate strategy? What new developments are taking place that will have a necessary product or process in them? How can we capitalize on that by becoming the sole sup-

plier/manufacturer/provider? Can we develop what we already do into a speciality skill that can be used to create a unique position in a new or developing industry? Do we have or can we acquire specialized market knowledge that we can use? Of which market(s) do we have knowledge that no one else has? Where lies our strongest market knowledge? Do you or your suppliers or customers complain about having to travel a long distance to get something? Do you have to use an out-of-town supplier to obtain something that should be available locally?

Calendar opportunities

Opportunities are often broadcast to the world via calendars, timetables, programme schedules and so on. Few people actually take these opportunities on board, unless the op is so visible that it can't help but be spotted. For instance many venues are already booked for New Year's Eve 1999. There will probably be a market in booked venue space operating during the lead up to the big date. Many street traders only operate during the big street functions (such as marches and carnivals). They studiously find out in advance what is taking place when and where. There will be opportunities for your company in the calendar. What significant events are coming up that you can capitalize on? What events will your customers need your help with?

Problem-led opportunity sources

- Mis-matches
- Opportunity-sensitive area
- Process needs
- Needs analysis
- Unexpected failure
- Re-definition of problem

Mis-match

What is a mis-match? It is a situation in which there is a lack of harmony or a discordance of some kind. There are five sources of opportunity that can be identified by the observation of a mis-match:

- Process or method mis-match
- Assumptions–reality mis-match
- Customer–provider value mis-match
- Economic mis-match
- Affordability mis-match

Process or method mis-match

In carrying out (for example) a four-step process, the perception of the quality of each stage could be expressed as: Smooth, Smooth, *Rough*, Smooth. That is the Rough part of the process 'feels' odd; it is out of step with the rest of the operation.

Seek processes in which some part feels

strange or incongruous with the rest of the process. Even if you personally are not involved in any of the processes you want to examine, you can rely on the perceptions of those in the front line. Front liners seem always to be acutely aware of those little problems. The visibility of different mis-matches will vary with the experience level of those carrying out the processes. Novices may feel awkward at some stages where the expert may not. Other problems may only be detectable by those with substantial experience. Cast a wide net when looking for process mis-matches.

Richard Duke was working in his family's garden centre when he noticed that customers felt uncomfortable about how exactly to use the pre-mixed lawn fertilizers they were buying. Despite instructions from Duke, customers came back to ask for more information. Duke had detected a process mis-match. He set up a company to provide lawn care. ChemLawn grew to a $49 million turnover in nine years.

Connor, a medical representative, was looking for an opportunity to establish his own business. By asking surgeons, he identified one part of eye surgery that caused concern. In senile cataract surgery, surgeons had to cut a ligament and tie blood vessels, thereby putting the eye at risk for a short but uncomfortable period during the operation.

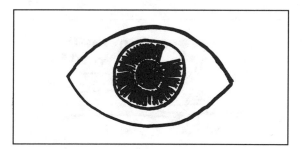

Speciality skill

Connor discovered that there was an enzyme known to dissolve this ligament, but that it had virtually no shelf-life. A brief research sortie into preservatives equipped Connor with a means of giving the enzyme sufficient shelf-life to be usable. The preserved ligament-dissolving compound removed the need to cut and tie, thereby massively improving eye surgery. Connor's compound removed the mis-match in senile cataract surgery. And needless to say made him a fortune.

What parts of a/the process do users complain

or feel uneasy about? What do novices experience as difficult or awkward? Which parts irritate the experts? Have you actively organized a search for areas of your business (or your customers' business) that create discomfort?

Assumptions–reality mis-match

The shipping industry assumed for years that costs were to be saved by having faster and faster ships with fewer and fewer people on them. Strenuous effort was applied to increase the financial effectiveness of ships while at sea.

In reality all the major problems were happening in the ports. Ships tied up in ports, not working, were what cost money. The time and delays spent in loading and stowing were where the expenses lay. There was a mis-match between assumptions and the reality of where costs were being incurred. The solution lay in separating loading from stowing to minimize the time spent in port: Ro-Ros and container storage were born!

In the UK, as the crime rate increased throughout the post-war years, the public demanded tough action. More people were sent to prison. The crime rate continued to rise. The public had assumed that prison was the answer, but it had the opposite effect. There was (and still is at time of writing) a mis-match between the

Mis-match: assumption – reality

assumptions about handling crime and reality.

In Germany, where a similar phenomenon had occurred, a series of studies revealed that the recidivism rate (33 per cent) for stern 'lock 'em up' judges was nearly 50 per cent greater than for milder 'education and community service' judges (23 per cent). Not only do the milder judges get better results, but their approaches cost about 10 per cent of their sterner colleagues' policies. Germany PLC is now making massive savings and getting better results in dealing with crime.

Are your efforts going to where the results can be found? Is the assumption you make about where results can be found sustainable? Identify all the assumptions behind the activity you are examining. Critically assess each assumption. Get others who are uninvolved to assess your assumptions.

Customer–provider value mis-match

The received, retail industry wisdom in Japan at the time TVs were being purchased *en masse* in the western world was: 'The poor in Japan will not buy a TV: it is an unnecessary luxury item'. However, they did buy TVs, *EN MASSE!* Why? Because even though they could not afford them, TVs gave value way beyond that which 'luxury items' usually provided. It provided access to a whole new world and indeed, for some, even changed their lives. There was a mis-match between the provider's perception of value and the customer's perception of value. This opportunity source can best be identified by the presence of arrogance in an industry.

While studying for a psychology degree, it occurred to me that the lecturers were not using psychological principles of learning to teach psychology. For instance, we know that entertaining information is much more easily remembered and understood. I asked a very senior lecturer (name deliberately excluded) why the department was not practising what it preached and was told 'We are lecturers, not entertainers!' Uh? Pursuing the point led to the discussion being terminated with a 'walk off' by the lecturer. There is an enormously lucrative market for entertaining trainers in just about any subject you care to mention. The lecturer concerned erected a barrier between himself and the opportunity, and alerted me to the potential at the same time.

When you hear 'We are . . ., we are not . . .', you

Mis-match: assumption – reality

Economic mis-match

know there is arrogance, and where there is arrogance, there is opportunity.

What arrogance is present in your industry? Where can you find the 'we know what the customer wants' attitude' Where have you heard marketing staff complain that the product or service is not quite what the client is looking for? In what businesses or other industries have you noticed that the efforts of management are not what you – as the customer – want?

Economic mis-matches

Health care in the developed countries provides an example. In the late 1920s, health care accounted for around 1 per cent of GNP, now it is 3 to 15 per cent. But costs have risen much faster than the service provided. Service has lagged behind costs. Demand is still growing and can't be supplied. The demand is potentially infinite. This creates a distinct opportunity and private health insurance companies, private hospitals and so on, are falling over themselves to fill it. How can you identify such an opportunity in your industry? Or in an industry you can supply?

In what growing businesses has service per unit of currency been falling when logic would dictate that economies of scale would have had the opposite effect? What businesses are becoming decreasingly profitable or are

increasingly unprofitable in an expanding market-size situation? Where are the new small businesses that are filling the increasing market? What are they doing that is different/better? What can you learn from your new, small competitors? Which businesses are becoming profitable in a shrinking market? Which parts of your business are being increasingly profitable in what others see as a shrinking market? Have you stumbled on an incongruity that you have unwittingly exploited? If so, what can you do to make your discovery even more profitable?

Affordability mis-match

Most people have many desire–means mismatches. Identifying what people want, but can't afford, or identifying what people want, but can't find an affordable version will hand you opportunities on a plate. Sir Clive Sinclair, the electronics wizard, used this strategy successfully on a number of occasions. He would invent the thing people wanted at a price they could afford. Many Japanese companies use this strategy too.

This strategy is strongly linked to the Needs analysis strategy and would probably be best used in conjunction with it.

Opportunity -sensitive area

This is an area of activity that seems ripe for new ideas. The area needn't be one in which there are massive problems. It could be drawn to your attention by a vague sense of 'something better could be going on here'.

Examples of sensitive areas: In 1992/3, UK public opinion seemed to be against closer European integration yet no political party opposed such a move. The UK manufacturing base seems to have been declining and becoming less competitive for several decades (in the face of massive undercutting by the developing countries) yet politicians seek to 're-build' the manufacturing base rather than 're-think' the national strategy in manufacturing. There is a shortage of hazardous waste dumping sites, yet there are many thousands of acres of contaminated land lying idle, and, the UK government has blocked attempts to compile a statutory register of contaminated land.

An opportunity-sensitive area can be identified by the presence of such feelings as; 'That's outrageous; we must be able to do better than that!' 'What a waste; it needn't be that way'. The absenteeism rate amongst western workers (particularly in public and health sector related jobs) is outrageously high. Here is an opportunity for improvement: how should you tackle it? A little library-based research would reveal that absenteeism in UK firms is twice as high as in Japanese companies. A sortie through the business research abstracts would uncover the reasons for the difference: more questioning of absentees – a formal interview on the day of return to work and so on. British firms that adopt the Japanese approach obtain similar results. A simple trip to the library on this opportunity could save you millions. If you are outraged, don't get mad: get educated.

Which areas of operation in other industries seem likely to respond significantly to ideas? Which are the areas of highest cost?

Which should be the areas of lowest cost, but are not? Are there areas in which there is a generalized feeling that further development needs to be done but is not being done? Are there areas (which are they?) in which specific problems exist and are widely known, but remain unaddressed by one and all?

Opportunity-sensitive areas

Process needs

All publishing technology by 1885 had become efficient – except typesetting. The same manual method from the 1400s was still being used. Everyone in the industry knew the publishing process needed faster and preferably automated typesetting. The need was so clear and strong that the industry immediately snapped up the 'linotype' invention of Mergenthaler.

The 'experts' were predicting that if telephone

Process needs

communication continued to expand at the rate it was expanding when it first became publicly accessible, half the population would be required to operate the system. The need for an automatic switching system was obvious.

Choose a specific process going on within an industry or business and ask: What need is being fulfilled and what is missing in the process that is seeking to fulfil it? How can the process be improved, revolutionized or avoided?

Focus on an individual task or process, one that is self-contained. What needs to be done? What is missing in the process? Where is the weak link? How can it be strengthened or avoided by new technology or with the new use of existing technology? Try looking at another task or process, then another . . .

Needs analysis/cat skinning

A 'need' is any want, desire, wish or fantasy that is being satisfied already or could be satisfied if you could find a way of doing so. It is also any product, process, task or event. Can a particular need be satisfied in other ways? The need to fly was well satisfied by the invention of the aeroplane. So why did we respond so positively to the invention of the helicopter? Well, the aeroplane requires a long strip of flat, hard land, close to wherever you want to leave from and close to wherever you want to go. By providing vertical flight the helicopter removes the need for a landing strip. It offers a different way of obtaining the same or very similar benefits.

Needs analysis

Those slightly different ways of skinning the cat contain opportunity. If you can provide a new, different or novel way of satisfying a universal human need (or even a localized need) you have a huge opportunity.

What are the universal human needs? Fortunately several great minds have been down this road before. Maslow's hierarchy, for instance, probably expresses and lists all needs and the order in which they will be fulfilled by most people:

1 Psychological needs: to satisfy hunger, thirst, shelter, copulatory needs.
2 Safety needs: to feel secure, safe and out of danger.
3 Belonging needs: to love, to join with others, to be accepted and to belong.
4 Esteem needs: to achieve, to be competent and to be approved of and perceived as such.
5 Intellectual needs: to know and acquire knowledge, to understand, and explore.
6 Aesthetic needs: to have symmetry, order and beauty in one's life and environment.
7 Self-actualization needs: to find self-fulfilment and to realize one's potential.

Which need should you address to find opportunities? Make a decision by listing them in order down the left-hand side of a large sheet of paper. Alongside each category of need, list five industries which aim to address it. To the right of that draw a 'typical customer' profile, a description of what kinds of people are seeking to satisfy that need. Which are you best equipped to address? Then start asking empowering questions.

In what ways is that need being currently satisfied? Is it being totally satisfied? How can that need be satisfied in other, preferably better ways? How many different ways can you devise to satisfy the need? Does the need exist because something else is lacking? Can you find a way to satisfy the lack that removes the consequent need?

Focus on any other need that takes your fancy. Choose one from the hierarchy, and try to satisfy it in a different way. Given the enormity of human need, this is a strategy you can come back to indefinitely!

The take-up rate of a newly provided opportunity will depend on the intensity of the need in the persons being addressed, and the extent to which the need is satisfied. You can analyse the intensity of need on an arbitrary basis using the following scale or, indeed, using any other similar scale you wish to construct:

1   Absolute Need
    Strong Need
2   Strong Desire
    Strong Wish
3   Wish
    Idle Fantasy

Intensity of Need

For instance, the take-up of the helicopter has been substantially greater in the military than it has been with the commercial world. Why? Because the military has an absolute need, whereas the commercial world has only a strong wish or preference.

The stronger a need the more of an opportunity there will be in satisfying it in a different way. Your efforts would therefore be most productive if aimed at seeking other ways of satisfying absolute needs with different products or services.

Unexpected failure/funny flops

When something goes unexpectedly wrong, find out why it failed. It's full of info! Drucker cites an excellent example of the builders in the USA in the mid-1970s who tried to sell the 'basic house' to young families. It was a dismal and unexpected failure. Unexpected because there was a shortage of affordable housing for the first batch of the baby boom generation. One astute firm realized that no one wanted to live in a basic or inferior standard house, but that the customer didn't mind living in his/her first house, or in a house that was able to be

Unexpected failure

upgraded as incomes improved. The builder had planning permission to extend the houses in various ways as and when the families required. It was a big success.

Unexpected failure? Find out why. It's full of info! If you notice anything going unexpectedly wrong in any industry, keep a note of it. Analyse these failures for useful info. What marketing reason was there for the failure? What production reason? A distribution, or any other discernible reason?

Re-definition of problem

The IX Problem (see Constraint Analysis, page 63) is easily solved when you either re-define it or analyse the constraints. Often the answer to a problem lies, not in the solution, but in the problem itself. Indeed the answer may be blatantly obvious after the problem is re-defined.

The Sinclair C5 turned out to be a terrible failure. Why? The problem had probably been ill-defined. The question or problem that was posed may have been: 'How can we provide a low-cost means of battery-powered transport?' The C5 does indeed answer this problem. But it didn't satisfy the customers.

When the problem is re-defined as follows, it

Re-definition of problem

stands more chance of success: 'How can we provide a low-cost means of transport that will keep people dry and that they feel safe using?'

Will re-defining the problem work? Watch the new Renault Zoom electric car to see. Re-definition can mean fine tuning a definition (of the problem) or completely changing perspective as in the case of the IX Problem.

Take a day-to-day problem with any industry. Try to re-define it. Question the question. Are you or others asking the right question? Can the problem be solved in a way other than the anticipated solution(s)? Does the problem exist at all if you look at the problem from other per-

Re-definition of problem

spectives? Which of the assumptions about the problem are sustainable? Which are not? What would happen if you altered the assumptions?

Re-defining the problem is very similar to the Challenge strategy. You could strengthen each by using them together.

Solution-led opportunity sources

- Bio-mimicry
- Tao tactics
- Better at both
- Bought in from abroad
- Tap into others' resources
- Symbiosis
- Piggybacking
- Network knitting
- Me too and creative imitation
- Unexpected success
- Problem solving
  - Standard solutions
  - Constructed solutions
- Transfer
- The something method
- Working backwards

Bio-mimicry

Nature is full of examples of great ideas which various creatures use to carve out a means of eating a living. We should be able to generate enough ideas to fill several hundred lifetimes simply by observing and choosing from the almost infinite variety of niche strategies available in the natural world. If you are, or ever have been, seriously interested in the natural world, this strategy could turn out to be your favoured Opportunity-Spotting method.

Humanity has generated many innovations using bio-mimicry: flight from imitating birds, underwater breathing apparatus from

mimicking sea mammals, radar from bats, Velcro from burrs . . . There are many imitations still being attempted. Various laboratories are trying to make a material similar to that from which spiders spin their webs (it is extremely strong, sticky, and recyclable).

Which phenomena in nature fascinated you,

recently or when you were a kid? Which abilities of which creatures do you envy? If you had the lifting power of an ant or the jumping power of a grasshopper, what could you achieve? Which creature can do . . . (what it is you want to achieve) and how does it do it? How can I copy or mimic that?

Tao tactics

The principle behind judo and many of the martial arts is to harness the opponent's force, not by controlling it but merely redirecting it. The same principle is part of the psyche of many Eastern cultures. Opportunity can be found by thinking of the way things happen naturally and asking empowering questions about how you can tune in to, ride along with, or slightly redirect the natural way of things. If you think it sounds a bit mystical, read on.

Of the known 'cancer cures' – removal, radiotherapy, chemotherapy, electrification – all are weak, unpredictable and unreliable. At worst, they are charlatanism behind a white coat. At best, they work on a hit or miss basis, or 'only when caught soon enough', (and by deduction if they don't work it wasn't the fault of the cure, but because 'it wasn't caught in time').

Compared to the strength, power and versatility of our own immune systems all other methods are second-rate. However it is the immune system's failure that permits the cancer to exist at all. The immune system fails to recognize the cancer cells, seeing them as part of its own body. In theory, all that needs to be done to eradicate a cancer is to develop some means of marking the cancer cells so the immune system can direct its power.

Experiments into this method have shown that removing cancer cells from mice, genetically altering them, and returning them allows the immune system to see and destroy the enemy. But – wait for it – the immune system is also able to see the *unaltered* cancer cells and destroys them too (tao?). This is by far the most promising of the future cancer treatments.

If you have been fighting some problem and your methods are not working or are working poorly, as has been the case in the human fight against cancer, choose to start working with nature. Look for ways to follow the natural course of events. A great judo throw is always based on your opponent's attempts to throw you. The Tao of Opportunity is using the natural forces that previously you fought against.

What problems have you been struggling with? Identify the natural forces at work behind these problems. How can you tune in to, ride along with, or redirect these forces in such a way that you solve your problem and achieve your goal?

Better at both (fastest with the best)

McDonald's is a classic example of fastest with the best. The company has grown on the basis of high and, perhaps more importantly, consistent quality. Hoffman La Roche (the Swiss drugs company) also owe their success to this strategy; in the 1920s they bought the patents and the best brains associated with the newly discovered vitamins and took them to market at incredible speed. They still dominate the market.

Although perhaps the best known of all innovative strategies, fame has not diminished its effectiveness. Like most strategies you need to keep using it or you'll lose the lead you obtained by it. You either have an ongoing policy of strategic evolution or you'll witness a sudden market-share revolution. The McDonald's and BurgerKing package remained unchanged for a long period. More than long enough for a competitor to come in under their noses.

Rally's, a new USA hamburger giant, used the fastest with the best strategy against the previously fastest with the best. Rally's CEO, Burt Sugarman, noticed that the industry giants were really not that fast, not if you were in a hurry and had little cash. He established the business on the basis of 'We get it right, or you get it free'. Getting it right involved delivering a full order chosen from only 11 items in a maximum time of 45 seconds on a drive-through or walk-up basis (no seating).

Rally's were fast enough and good enough to capture a $100 million share of the market coming in from 400+ outlets.

How can you make the product better, faster, and more appealing to the customer? Are there any unusual ways you can improve the customers' perception of the product/service? How can you alter customer perception of 'fast' or 'best' without altering the product? Try regularly to define the 'success characteristics' of other people's products/services (as defined by customers). How can you fulfil these success characteristics better, easier, cheaper, quicker . . .? How do your own customers define your successful performance? (Ask them!)

Bought in from abroad

This strategy aims to find opportunity by importing successful overseas products/services/methods. It is best used by focusing on one industry or business at a time. The UK pizza industry boom in the 1980s and 1990s was based on this strategy. In fact, before pizzas were imported from the USA to the UK they were imported into the USA from Italy.

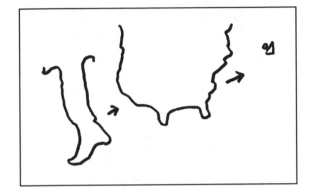

Brought in from abroad

Anita Roddick's Body Shop was founded on this strategy. While travelling around the world, on a year off, she learned how the women of various tribal societies cleansed and moisturized their skin. She thought the methods used might go down well at home. Several hundred shops worldwide later, it appears she might have been right.

Alan Sainsbury had similar thoughts. The UK supermarket chain which still carries the family name was founded when Alan Sainsbury went to the USA just after the first supermarkets started appearing there. He brought the idea home with him.

What products or services are being provided abroad, but not here? Or which are being provided here but not as well as the customer really wants them? Or not as well as they are being provided abroad? Which products are being provided here but not abroad? How can you be sure the product's absence isn't a cultural phenomenon rather than a product/market deficiency?

Tap in to others' resources

Each country and company seems to have its own special expertise. There is nothing new

about poaching another company's or even other country's human resources. What is new is the scale the poaching has taken on recently. Many companies are seeing and acting on the opportunities available for poaching a country's intellectual giants simply by setting up a research base in that country and under the gamekeepers' noses. It is the international level equivalent of setting up your competitive analysis section in your main competitor's HQ!

In an age when intellectual resources are becoming more sought after than physical resources, the world's industrial giants – Japan and the USA – are setting up research labs in each other's back yards. Eastman Kodak, IBM, Du Pont, DEC, Pfizer, to name but a few, have research bases in Japan employing Japanese brains. The Koreans, too, have adopted this strategy. Samsung decided to move into the chips (semiconductors) market in 1983, so they set up a research lab where? Yes, you've guessed, in San Jose, California. Samsung then had open access to the intellectual resources of the best in the industry.

Moonlighting employees are willing to offer their expertise (naturally without breaking any laws) to the highest bidder. Nine years later, $2 billion of Samsung's £8 billion revenues comes from semiconductors. In 1993 they led the entire industry with their innovative 64MB memory chip. Unbelievably: 0–$2 billion + industry leadership in ten years. Tapping into others' resources is a pretty powerful strategy!

Which company or country has resources you would like to use? How can you gain access to them? If your competitors have what appears to be an overwhelming advantage, ask yourself empowering questions about how you can utilize the advantage rather than being devastated by it.

Symbiosis/synergy/gestalt/partnership strategy

The joining of forces in the plethora of possible ways comes and goes as a favoured, or otherwise, strategy with the whims of fashion. It should not be ignored. Some of the greatest successes in innovation and commercial history have come from individual people deciding that the whole created by teaming up with others would be greater than the sum of their individual parts (a gestalt).

The Laura Ashley company, despite the name, was a wife and husband team. This strategy is similar to Tap in to others' resources, but is different in that both parties consent to do so.

Many of the country's commercial success stories could only have happened in a partnership or symbiotic relationship of one kind or another. To name only a few UK-based examples: Hanson and White (Hanson Plc), Saatchi & Saatchi, Stirling and Bruce (P&O).

Many partnerships form by accident or by birth, but some are the result of deliberate and conscious decisions to combine component skills to create a larger, more effective whole.

Which resource would you like access to? Who would like access to your resources? How can you form a mutually beneficial arrangement? There are plenty of examples of this strategy working in nature, for instance the Clown Fish forms a mutually protective relationship with a species of anemone. Perhaps you can combine this strategy with Bio-mimicry and look for innovative opportunities by copying nature's partnerships.

Piggybacking

Piggybacking (a kid's game in which one party hitches a lift on the back of the other) is a much used but distinct variety of the synergy strategy. The opportunity is obtained by piggybacking someone else's operation in such a way that having you on their back benefits them.

Ted Turner made Channel 17 (Atlanta, USA) a big success by piggybacking the cable television systems America-wide. Nothing exciting now, but then it was a big opportunity waiting for the first innovator to come along.

Avis persuaded many of the USA airlines to carry his airport-based car rental advertising cards in their aircraft seat pockets. The airlines benefited by being able to make the use of their service easier for customers (they could get to and from airports with greater ease), and Avis benefited from highly targeted marketing.

What existing operations could you benefit from if you could find a way to piggyback them? OK, now devise at least two possible ways to do so. Take each component of your business operation, and ask yourself what you'd like to be able to piggyback for each. Next find a way to do so.

Network knitting

Network knitting is a variation on the previous two strategies, but can be used independently. Identify an existing network or grouping that you can knit your product or service into. The benefits of being part of a larger group are many, ranging from enhanced buying and selling power to the power obtained by the formation of industry standards, to protectionism, to . . .

Many companies have faced decisions to prosper or perish on the basis of joining or not joining a network. DEC (USA) joined the Open Software Foundation (after years of refusal) so that its VAX system could be made more valu-

able through the increased accessibility it would acquire by being knitted to other systems.

Some astute companies have even gone as far as creating networks in order to gain market dominance. JVC made its VHS technology widely available to almost anyone who wanted to manufacture it. They now have a virtual worldwide monopoly in video systems.

What networks are there in your industry or business? What networks are there in other industries? In what ways could you knit in to your own industry's or other industries' networks? What networks could you set up to strengthen your own position?

Me too, and creative imitation

This strategy is about jumping on a bandwagon when someone else has invented it (and taken all the risks), established the market and started it rolling. The 'first there' party has to recover their development costs – you don't! You can therefore charge less. Further you can use their finished product/service as your starting point. Samsung's entry into the chip market can be seen in terms of this strategy. Whether or not Samsung management planned to obtain the benefits of 'Me too' they did, and in a historically big way. (See Tap others' resources for details.)

Use the competition's end point as the point from which to start. Seek improvements in production costs, quality, marketing . . . It is widely held that the Japanese success story can be attributed (at least partially) to their ability to make growth area products cheaper than anyone else (after someone else has started the ball rolling and/or established a market).

The strategy is not peculiar to Eastern cultures. The one-time American giant Pan Am was founded by Juan Trippe after the embryo airline industry had been established. He could see the profit potential as industry growth accelerated.

Which current bandwagons could you jump

Me too/creative imitation

on? Which products or services are selling well that you could make or provide? Could you make or provide a close substitute? Can you conceive of a slightly better or more appealing version of the same thing? Could you provide it? Can you come up with a way to produce/provide the same thing more cheaply than the original inventor(s)?

Unexpected success

This strategy alerts you to opportunity when something positive or beneficial happens that couldn't have or shouldn't have, in other words, when the unexpected happens in the most unexpectedly favourable manner.

The early IBM bookkeeping machine was sold to, indeed was for sale only to, banks. It was thought no one else would have the use for or the funds to buy one. During a depression in that market, a librarian commented to Thomas Watson that his sales manager had refused to demonstrate the machine to her. When Watson did demonstrate it and did sell it, a whole new market opened up. The rest is history.

While running a milk shake machine company, Ray Kroc discovered that one of his customers, a restaurant in California, had bought eight of his machines. That was many more than anyone else. Ray Kroc was alerted to an opportunity by this unexpected success. He went to investigate and found a team of brothers running a very successful business but with no

Unexpected success

ambition or inclination to expand. Kroc saw the opportunity, negotiated for and bought a franchise licence. The rest of the story can be seen on virtually every high street in the world: McDonalds.

As with unexpected failures, keep a note of things that go well, accidental discoveries and so on. In what sectors has there been progress that was not anticipated? Have any products suddenly started selling well for no apparent reason? Has any company out-performed all the others inexplicably? Where have there been positive results that you and your colleagues would not have predicted? What is it about the unexpected success that contains opportunity? Has any customer bought much more of your output than anyone else?

Problem solving

Standard solutions

Doctors, lawyers, dentists all solve your problems by applying standard solutions to standard problems. Often non-standard problems in one field can be solved by taking standard solutions from another. For instance medicine regularly 'pinches' engineering solutions to solve biological problems.

How can you gather standard solutions from other disciplines? It is worth making occasional journeys into unfamiliar territory. The world's top chemical scientists struggled for months to identify the configuration of carbon-60. The solution was widely available, but it was not until a mathematics professor was consulted that they discovered the structure was that of a common or garden soccer ball – a widely available standard solution, to say the least.

Examine the solutions you have to a particular problem or set of problems. How can these solutions be applied to other as yet unsolved problems? Compile a list of standard solutions Seek to apply those to other problems, other contexts, other industries.

Make a list of unsolved problems and seek standard solutions from other disciplines, industries or even other departments. Can the methods you use to monitor debtor days be used to monitor communication lags between departments (as an example)? Look at solutions you think are attractive or could have wider appeal and seek to apply those to other

Problem solving

Transfer

problems and to other contexts.

Constructed solutions

In areas of human endeavour where new ground has to be broken, solutions often have to be constructed. Those new solutions then find applications in other areas. In the development of manned spaceflight, several constructed solutions found their way to the market as innovations. Behind each innovation coming to market, there is someone who saw the opportunity and went for it. Almost certainly that person identified a way to use the new solution in other contexts.

Break down any problem you have into sub-problems and from that construct a solution. (This is one of the things most executives are paid to do.) The difference here is each time you do this, ask: To which other areas could this constructed solution be applied? Or more appropriately, since this is the External opportunities section, look at other industries or businesses. Which of their constructed solutions has potential use to you or your business/industry?

Transfer

Kompass (a UK publication) was originally developed as a buyers' guide but is now sold mainly to sellers. The transfer of a sail from a dinghy on to a surfboard started a whole new business: the wind-surfing business. The technology to create that new business has been with us for over 150 years, yet it was only recently that the transfer strategy (or possibly the convergence of technology strategy) was applied to the coastal leisure business.

The latest transfer to affect the windsurfer was made by A level student, James Harvey. He transferred the concept of the catamaran to the windsurfer, creating a twin-hulled version which is just as fast and easier to sail than a single board.

How many other businesses could benefit from this strategy? More directly, how could your business benefit from Transfer? Look at the processes (as opposed to solutions) in other industries and businesses: how can they be transferred to your industry? The more bizarre the jump/transfer the better. Choose an industry and review its processes one by one, trying to apply each to your own business. In the vast majority of cases where no transfer is possible, what ideas does the attempt stimulate? How can you use those ideas in another context to make more sense?

The something method

Define the characteristics of a solution you desire and start looking for something to help you achieve your end point. If your cat is stuck on your roof, you need something to get up on to and down from the roof, with the cat – a ladder, scaffolding . . .

The something method

To find opportunity with this strategy, define and list the characteristics of some end point you'd like to reach. For example, 'I'd like to find some way of improving the performance of admin. staff by linking reward to performance'. We have defined the characteristics sufficiently vaguely so that several possibilities could satisfy them.

Using vague words makes your range of possible solutions wider than specific words would. Note in the example the use of vague words like 'performance', 'admin. staff', 'linking', 'reward' (as opposed to specifically: 'pay', 'promotion' . . .). Compile a list of possibilities that could satisfy each characteristic. Generate innovative solutions by sequentially pulling together different possible satisfiers of each characteristic into an overall package. Bring together the possible satisfiers in different combinations until you have generated some ideas.

Working backwards/end-state method

Start the opportunity search from a highly specified definition of the desired end-state (not characteristics as above). For example the desired end-state from the cat on the roof problem is the cat safely on the ground. A loud

Working backwards

recording of a dog barking from the attic space can work wonders for a cat's motivation to return to earth.

Work backwards from the very specifically defined end-state, not from a proposed solution. You are trying to find a/the solution(s) that will take you there. Having defined your end-state, see how many different solutions will achieve the same goal.

Some example questions: How can I get the cat down from the roof? How can I get the cat TO come down from the roof? How can I get the cat off the roof (not necessarily to the ground)?

Exercise reminder: Have you devised two additional questions for each of the strategies so far presented?

2

Internal Sources

Internal opportunities are those that can be found by looking at sources inside the company/organization or individual. There is a considerable overlap in the use of the various strategies. Many, maybe most, strategies can be used to find opportunities internally or externally. Some have been included in both chapters. An exercise at the end of the section asks you to find strategies in each chapter that could be used in both. You needn't wait until the end of the chapter; you could consider how each internal method could be used as an external strategy as you go through.

There are three categories of internal opportunity. As usual categories are purely descriptive and are not in any way absolute boundaries.

- Self-observation opportunity sources
- Problem-led opportunity sources
- Solution-led opportunities sources

Self-observation

- Navel gazing and empowerment
- Unused assets
- Unique skills combination
- Skills audit
- Customer experience
- Process assets
- Situational assets
- Challenge
- Alchemy of anger
- What business are we in
- Mis-match

Navel gazing and empowerment

Empowering is/was one of the management buzz-words in the early 1990s. Examining your own operation can generate all sorts of opportunities, especially if the people who know most about your organization – the staff – carry out the navel gazing exercise. The process can be even more opportunity-rich if the staff are empowered with the knowledge that their ideas will be listened to and taken seriously by top management. Empowerment may be just another management buzz-word cynically used by some to demonstrate they are 'on the ball and in control', but some companies have taken the combination of navel gazing and empowerment very seriously and obtained great results.

The American and international giant, GE, have realized that analytical managers do not have a monopoly on ideas and have introduced three idea generating and gathering strategies.

Workout

A workout is a place or forum where the participants can make any of three things happen:

1 have a mental workout, a brainstorming session;
2 take unnecessary work out of their job descriptions;
3 or work out specified problems together.

The participants bash away at their agenda for two days, at the end of which the CEO returns and is permitted only one of three rapid responses to the generated ideas: Yes, no, or more information please. The rapid response to suggestions is designed to handle the genuine concerns of employees that ideas can be easily buried or stalled, or never acted on by anyone in the chain of command between them and the CEO.

There are two major weakness in GE's strategy. One is that the boss sets the agenda (thereby missing out on a goldmine of information from his/her staff) and the second is that staff members at the workouts are chosen by managers – thereby missing out on a goldmine of information from other, perhaps more idea-productive, staff. Self-selecting group members are usually more motivated.

Best practices

The method used is virtually the same as the Bought in from abroad strategy except that instead of foreign countries, other manufacturers and other divisions within the same company are selected. GE gathers information on what are the best practices. There are many benefits to be obtained from this strategy besides the possibility of coming up with a great opportunity: it helps managers counter-act the natural tendency to focus on outcomes while being less aware of the effect processes have on those outcomes.

Process mapping

A modern version of what was time and motion study, the difference now is that employees are empowered to look for and implement savings and improvements in the way they do their jobs. Staff now take pride in doing a good job; they can control the processes and output within their sphere of influence; they are recognized for their thinking power. After years of having their intellectual resources ignored, workers have been reward-ed rather than penalized for bringing their minds to the workplace.

The performance effect of the empowerment philosophy in GE has increased productivity by 6 per cent. But the real benefit will take longer to come through. It will probably show itself in terms of absenteeism rates dropping, retention rates increasing, quality of staff improving . . .

Unused assets

Opportunities can be found where there is unused potential. For instance, a piece of land that could obtain more valuable planning permission than its current use has unused potential. Similarly with people, if you conduct a skills audit on all of your staff, you'll find a staggering array of skill, knowledge and talent

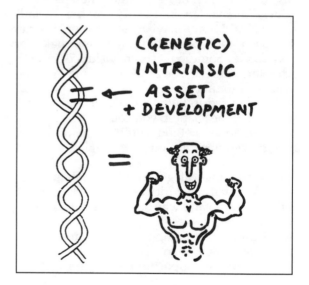

that someone somewhere is probably already paying a fortune for. Although the assets uncovered may not be in your business area, can you afford to ignore them? Are you using your assets fully? Could they be used in other ways? By other people (variable value)? Have you specialist knowledge that has asset value if used properly? What failures have you had recently that give you knowledge that you would not otherwise have had? Do you have land, property, location, equipment, people, market position and so on that can be of value if used by others or if used by you in a different way or place or time?

Perhaps you could start by listing all your assets, material, situational and so on. Ask staff members: What do we have that could be better used? Perhaps you could compile an 'Unused or under-used assets questionnaire' and distribute it to all staff for completion.

Skills audit strategy

How would a CEO feel if s/he had paid a translations firm tens of thousands of what-ever currency only to find that s/he had two or three or more fluent speakers or even native speakers of the language concerned on the payroll of the company, in some other capacity? Pretty dim? How would they feel if a few members of staff were professional or serious amateur photographers after spending a fortune on photographic services provided externally? Less than smart? You can be sure that many companies are currently paying for expertise outside that they already have, virtually free, in-house.

Has your personnel department ever conducted a skills audit and compiled a company skills database? If they do, you'll discover that an amazing list of skills, knowledge and talent are already on your payroll. Most people have skills in several areas, only a few of which you will see them bringing to work.

The opportunities contained in the newly compiled database could keep you going in ideas for a very, very long time. You could empower your staff to do the skills combining for you by inviting them to brainstorming meetings where they can discuss how to combine their skills to create opportunities for the company. You are already paying your staff to make their skills available to the company; how can you help them to get closer to reaching their potential while benefiting the company?

Unique skills combination

Combining two or more skills in a unique way can create opportunities. Richard Dennis combined investment knowledge with computer know-how to make a fortune from investing. Apply the principle to yourself.

1 List all your skills down one side of a page.
2 Photocopy the page.
3 Put the second page on top of the first so you can see both lists.
4 Focus on one skill on the left-hand list and slowly slide the contents of the other list past in such a way that you combine one skill with all the others.
5 As each pair is created, ask yourself what service or product and benefits to others the combination could provide.
6 Make a third copy of the list and do the same with combinations of three skills.

Customer experience strategy

The customer experience strategy aims to direct you to the opportunities contained in your customers' changing level of experience with your product or service. What a customer wants from a product will change as they have experience of its use. Naive, first-time, or occasional users will have different requirements from sophisticated or regular users. And as/if

41

customers move up the learning curve their requirements will change.

Customers know that their needs will change. Some buyers of computers will check that there is an expansion or upgrade route available with the machine. For others, expansion is not an issue; they assume that by the time their needs have changed, the technology will be so outdated as to be not worth upgrading. Still others ignore the manufacturers' promises because they know the rapid progress of technology will make the machines so rapidly obsolete that it makes manufacturers' well-intentioned commitments to provide upgrade continuity slightly less than worthless.

REALLY SIMPLE IDIOT CAMERA

HUGELY SOPHISTICATED 'PHD PHOTOGRAPHY' EQUIPMENT

Opportunity is more credibly found in responding to customers' changing experience level. Many providers of psychological tests provide a total support service for first-time users and have a decreasing service charge as the customer becomes more expert in administering and managing the tests independently.

Draw up an experience profile of your typical average customer from first contact to mature/sophisticated user level. From that, devise and add a section to your database that can be used to assess your customers' experience level on the basis of their previous orders. Set up a means of cross-referencing customer order history with your experience profile. The end result should enable you to predict when and for what the customer will need to place their next order, on the basis of their previous

orders. You can then make timely sales calls.

Process/operating assets

All processes, systems and methods have hidden, as well as openly intended, advantages and disadvantages. All – even apparently harmful – operating patterns can contain assets. For instance, despite the damage to physical and mental health done by heavy alcohol consumption, its key assets are social contact, dis-inhibition, and immediate relaxation.

Functional /operating asset

What systems, procedures and methods do you have? List them. Which are unique or peculiar to your company? Which are rare or unusual? What assets can you see in them? What assets do others see in them? Could your sales staff be selling other companies' products/services to your existing customers? Is your debt-collecting department so good that it may be worth setting it up as a separate company and offering the service to others? Is your advertising and marketing department so inept that they get publicity through their notoriety? What is there about the way you operate that contains invisible assets?

Circumstantial assets

The recent period (1989–92) of high interest rates in the UK proved a boom time for some:

Circumstantial asset

for example, investors locked into long-term high-interest savings accounts. Similarly, the situation in the mop-up after Operation Desert Storm allowed many fire-fighting teams to have their best business period ever (putting out oil well fires). The early 1990s recession made liquidation and receivership one of the most profitable businesses to be in at that time.

Highly profitable situations that others benefit from make it extremely tempting to follow the bandwagon strategy. However, beware of the risks of making long-term financial commitments to what must be a short-term situation. The recent (late 1980s) and extremely costly lesson of the big UK finance houses getting involved in what was a short-term boom in estate agency serves to illustrate.

Property booms are always short term. The heads of these companies knew that. But the profits looked so appealing that normal reasoning seemed to evaporate, taking with it hundreds of millions of pounds. Some have even made *post hoc* rationalizations to cover their backs, saying things like 'Of course we could see the short-term risks, but it was our long-term strategy to give our financial products the highest possible exposure at the most frequent point of sale: purchasing a house'. Ho

hum! Shortly before they sold the agencies at huge losses.

Nonetheless, all situations have assets and examining them can pay.

What new situations have developed or are developing that you can capitalize on? Have some or other circumstances affected the market in which you operate in any way? List the new situations you know about and find out about others you don't. For whom (which industries) could these circumstances create opportunities? Are any of these opportunities useful to you? How can you benefit indirectly from those situations you don't want to exploit, or don't want to expose yourselves to?

Challenge (internally)

Conventionally the skeleton of a building has been an integral part of the structure. Challenging that convention led to the external skeleton structure. Such a development allows much more space to be provided internally. One of the many possible examples is the NEC in the West Midlands, UK.

The 'You old fool' mentality can be constructive if directed with a few well-chosen questions. What do you regularly criticize about the *status quo* in your company? What could you challenge about that which seems OK? Look at

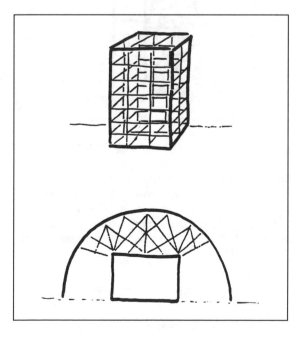

Challenge

all the systems, procedures and so on, and challenge them. Which areas are working so well that no one would think to challenge them to see if improvements or whole new methods could be used? Nothing should be exempt from challenge – least of all that which seems above reproach. Critically assess all the assumptions on which any procedure/system/department/product . . . is based.

The alchemy of anger

This strategy could have been called Fruitful frustration. We know that the only reason we get angry is that we didn't get our own way. Anger in business is regularly perceived as a loss of control, yet all of us get angry at home and elsewhere – especially when we are the customer.

If you get angry, it is because something you think ought to be happening isn't. Therein lies the opportunity. If you are not getting your own way, you can raise an opportunity instead of your blood pressure. Ask yourself why you are getting angry and say 'There is an opportunity in this frustration somewhere: where is it?'

What business are we in

The most famous example of this strategy is the head of a famous watch manufacturing

What business are we in

company, Rolex, declaring that they were not in the watchmaking business but the luxury business. Are car-makers in the transport or the freedom business? Are they in the image or the luxury business?

Is your perception of what you provide the same as your customers? What business do your colleagues think you are in? Are the benefits for which your customers buy your product the same benefits you think you are providing? Are you in the time-piece or the luxury business, the transport or status symbol business, the security or peace of mind business?

Phrase your question like that: Are we in the . . . or the . . . business? Once you have identified what business you are really in, opportunities for improvements in production, marketing and so on will become obvious. Or at least more obvious than they would be otherwise, without your new greater sense of direction.

Mis-matches

The route to opportunity in this strategy is as before in the external opportunity sources section, except this time you are seeking internal mis-matches. Opportunities can be found in the same four categories of mis-matches:

● Process mis-match
● Assumptions–reality mis-match

- Customer–provider mis-match
  Where the customer is a department which receives a service or product from another department.
- Economic mis-match
  Where each profit centre is seen as a business in its own right.

Process mis-match

It feels: smooth, smooth, *rough*, smooth. Look at all the processes/systems that you have in your company. Are there any processes that users complain or feel uneasy about? Have you actively organized a search for areas of your business (or the interface with your customers'

Process mismatch

business) that create discomfort for your staff or your clients? Are there any parts of your production or service delivery that regularly cause bottlenecks or delays, problems, resentment, stress tension, idle periods and so on, no matter how small?

Assumptions–reality mis-match

Are your efforts going to where the results can be found? Are the assumptions you make about where results can be found sustainable? Is the mission statement of each department consistent with where real results are to be found? Do the people in charge of that department actually carry out the mission statement or is it paid lip-service with efforts going elsewhere?

Customer–provider value mis-match

The mis-match can occur in several ways, for instance the customer may be receiving more value than you are aware of (Japanese TV 'revolution'). You may therefore be underpricing the product/service. Conversely, the customer may not be getting the value from the product you think it is being sold to obtain. Or you may simply be overestimating how much the product is worth to the customer.

Is there an arrogance in your company that 'we' know what the customer wants without actually ever having asked the customer, or at least not asked the customer recently? Do your marketing staff complain that the product or service is not quite what the client is looking for? Have you noticed any other competitor businesses where the efforts of management are not what the customers want? Where have you heard 'the customer is unwilling to pay for quality'? Here is where there is a gap between what the customer wants and what the business is providing. The opportunity is in balancing out a previously imbalanced or mis-matched situation.

Economic mis-match

A bit of repetition here. There should be a slightly different emphasis in your questions when you are applying the Economic mis-match strategy to the internal opportunity search. Make the word 'business' interchangeable with 'division', department' and 'section', when you are thinking of 'markets' in this context. Picture the other departments/divisions and so on that are effectively customers.

Are you in a business that is unprofitable in an

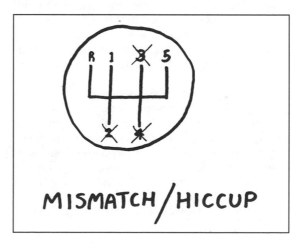

Mis-match: how it feels

increasing market-size situation? Where are the new small businesses that are filling this demand? What are they doing that is different/better? How can you capitalize on the gap between your reality and the markets? Is your business becoming profitable in a shrinking market? Have you stumbled on an incongruity that you have unwittingly exploited? If so, what can you do to make your discovery even more profitable? Are you, and you alone, selling enormously more of a product than you anticipated, or substantially less? Why are the costs of some departments rising while their performance is falling, or vice versa? Is some economic change happening when other measures are going in the opposite direction?

Problem-led opportunity sources

- Disadvantage into advantage
- Focus on area of weakness
- Process need
- Personal need
- Opportunity-sensitive area
- Information innovation
- Re-definition of problem
- Anticipatory problem avoidance
- War-gaming
- Unexpected failures
- Grow by shrinking

Disadvantage into advantage

The strategy here is to turn adversity into victory. One salmon canner had great difficulty selling its product because of the paler salmon colour than customers expected. Clearly the pale colour was a disadvantage. The company then marketed the product as 'the only pale salmon' and had great success! The company made 'paleness' a unique brand identifier thereby turning disadvantage into advantage.

This strategy can also be used with other sources of disadvantage. Perhaps there is an operating problem, a production problem, a finance or personnel problem. One enterprising computer company turned the disadvantage of skilled female employees leaving the workforce to have families by setting up a 'homeworkers scheme'. People now actively apply for these jobs because of the advantages involved.

What disadvantages does your product/ser-

Disadvantage into advantage

vice have? List them. What adverse events have happened to your company recently? How can you turn these 'problems' into assets? How can you re-package or re-present that product or service in a light that will sell it to those who either don't mind the 'disadvantage' or indeed actively seek it out? Can you generate some publicity from your 'problem'?

Focus on area of weakness

If you are in a business that has, as one of its major costs, the disposal of some waste product, the overheads associated with that are a weakness. But if you can find someone who views your waste as his/her raw material, you have turned your area of weakness into an asset.

Equally if you can find some use for your waste, you can turn weakness into strength. 'Area of weakness' is slightly different from 'disadvantage into advantage' in that you don't seek out active disadvantages; you look for milder problems or relative weaknesses. Indeed your area of weakness may even be identified by an absence of strength.

Could being understaffed in your accounting department be an opportunity to improve your accounting methods in such a way that you need fewer staff?

Could temporary production or supply weakness which alters or limits your output be an

Focus on area of weakness

Process needs

opportunity for a 'limited edition' promotion? Could your strapped marketing budget be an opportunity to acquire better PR (Public/Press Relations) skills? Could weakness in your . . . department be an opportunity to . . .?

Identify the areas in which your company is weak or is lacking in strength. Is it finance, marketing, production . . .? Which specific section is the source of the weakness?

Ask your staff for their views on weakness areas. How can these weaknesses be viewed as opportunities?

Process need

Your attention will probably be attracted to a process need opportunity by some problem or other within a process. Perhaps you will notice an opportunity by the desired consequence of a process not being achieved.

Perhaps a bottleneck keeps occurring in some process, or perhaps the quality of output is inconsistent. For example, when water-melons are large enough for harvesting, the conventional way to assess ripeness was to tap each melon by hand and listen to the noise made. The process is slow and inconsistent. There was a clear need for the process to be changed.

Now an automatic knocker is available; it drops a small weight from a fixed distance and the sound profile generated is digitally analysed. The outcome can be used to direct each melon to an appropriate destination.

Any spotted opportunity may only be for a minor improvement of sorts. But equally there comes a time where fine-tuning of a process must stop and a whole new process to achieve the same end must be instituted. A time when evolution ends and revolution begins.

You can also use this strategy without being dependent on process inadequacies to act as opportunity prompting cues by choosing to focus on any individual task or process that is of interest to you. It should always be a process that is self-contained. You would then ask the following kinds of questions. What is the objective of the process? What needs to be done? What's missing in the process that makes it imperfect? Where is the weak link? Can it be strengthened or avoided by new technology or with the new use of existing technology? Try looking at another task or process, then another . . .

Personal need or interest

If you need something that is not being provided, the chances are that others will need the same thing. Providing that something is the

Opportunity-sensitive area

source of opportunity. A young wartime pilot could never get ground-based transport when he arrived at the various places worldwide where his combat duties took him. He knew of the Hertz rent-a-car concept and wondered if the same idea could be applied purely at airports. Warren Avis set up what became a huge company.

What needs do you have that are not being satisfied? What unsatisfied needs do you regularly hear others complaining about?

Doctors Jan and Robert Knight were both interested in a peculiar shellfish called the piddock. This 'photo-genetic' rock-boring creature gives off light when irritated. The Knights were personally interested in this phenomenon. Their research led them to realize that there are medical applications of a safe fluorescent substance. They isolated the chemical which they called Pholasin and sought medical applications. They found them, and at the time of writing, the testing kits are on trial in France.

What personal interests do you have? In what ways could you look for a commercial application of that interest?

Opportunity-sensitive area

As before, you'll be attracted to an opportunity-sensitive area by some vague sense of 'something better could be happening here'. This strategy is distinct from the previous disadvantage and weakness strategies in that it is

drawn to your attention by the positive expectation contained in 'something better . . .'. Current opportunity-sensitive areas on a national scale are: drug use/abuse, car theft, inflation management, ERM (Europe only) . . .

At an internal level, many companies are finding better ways to manage their recruitment of new staff. One daring British company – B&Q (a DIY retailer) – has an active policy of recruiting only the 50+ age-group in some stores. The policy has proved so extremely successful with high productivity, higher levels of customer service and satisfaction, lower levels of absenteeism and lower staff turnover levels, shorter and cheaper training periods, avoidance of the demographic shift problem (increasing average age of western populations), that the company is extending the policy. Several other companies are looking seriously at this opportunity at the time of writing.

Look at areas of activity that seem ripe for new ideas (not just problem areas). Which areas of operation in your company seem likely to respond significantly to ideas? Which areas of activity have been unchanged for over two years? Which systems have not been tailored, altered or improved for over 1 year? Which are the areas of highest cost? Which should be the areas of lowest cost but are not? Are there areas in which there is a generalized feeling that furin which there is a generalized feeling that further development could be done, but is not being done? Are there areas (which are they?) in which specific problems exist?

Information innovation

As more and more information is kept and stored by all sorts of people, the generation of increasingly predictive information is possible. If you can find a way to gather. process or provide information that is needed or would be needed if only people knew it was available, you can open a gushing opportunity pipeline.

It must be noted that this strategy is not dependent on information technology. In the nineteenth century, Allan Pinkerton made a fortune from setting up files in his private investigations company. He logged information on known criminals, known associates, *modus operandi* and so on. While that may now seem obvious and even simple information to gather, for its time it was an enormous information-gathering innovation. And it proved to be a wealth-making opportunity for Pinkerton.

A more recent information-processing innovation can be seen in the computer industry's RISC (Reduced Instruction Set Code) technology. RISC works on the basis that 80 per cent of computer operations use only 20 per cent of the available instruction codes. By cutting down the number of codes available to the basic 20 per cent, the speed of a machine can be increased dramatically. The removed operations can be carried out via combinations of the

remaining codes. If you are a facts freak, this type of strategy is for you.

What information do you currently gather? Which information is available to you, but you don't gather? Ungathered information may be useless in itself. Gathering and combining it with what would make it useful? Do an 80:20 analysis on the information that is most frequently used by you or in your company generally. Determine the 20 per cent of information that makes up 80 per cent of that accessed. How can you make access to the core information faster, easier . . .? In what ways could you provide the required high-level information by combining simple easily-accessed portions of the whole?

Re-definition of problem

As before, but applied to internal problems. So you might wish to re-define your marketing problem from 'How do we get it to market?' to

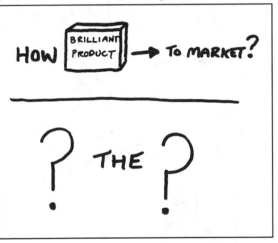

Re-definition of problem: question the question

'How do we get the market to come to us?' For example retail versus mail-order methods.

Take a day-to-day problem within your company. Challenge it. Question the question. Are you or others asking the right question? Can the problem be solved in a way other than the anticipated solution(s)? Does the problem exist at all if you look at the problem from other perspectives? Are the assumptions about the problem sustainable? What would happen if you altered the assumptions?

Anticipatory problem avoidance

This opportunity source strategy is similar to process need (look for a way to carry out a process without the problems), but is very different in that you look for a way of achieving the result of the process without the process! In other words if you have a faulty component, don't replace it – avoid the need to have it! This is the policy NASA use. You might find it more memorable to think of this strategy as being *process avoidance*.

If the water inlet to your factory was being polluted by the outlet of a factory upstream of you, there are several choices you can make to solve the problem (legal action, filtration and so on). Or you can completely avoid the problem by moving your water inlet upstream of

Process/problem avoidance

the pollution source. The strategy can create opportunities by avoiding a problem either in terms of geographical location, or timing, or . . .

In some countries, it is law that factories using rivers must have their inlet pipes downstream of their discharge pipes. The pollution problem is anticipated and avoided by the source of pollution by imposing a strong need not to pollute.

Which problems do you have that could be solved if something further back in the

process/sequence could be changed? Can the problem be avoided by totally removing that part of the process and replacing it with something else? Or can you dispense with that part of the process altogether? Could the introduction of a time delay create opportunity, or perhaps the removal of a delay?

Unexpected failures

Milk gone off, with the aid of bacteria, makes yoghurt. Failure of any sort always contains

Unexpected failure

valuable information and valuable opportunity. Inherent in the cause of unexpected failure is some new event or some hidden gem that was previously invisible to you.

Unexpected failure may give you the opportunity directly or indirectly. It came indirectly for Conrad Hilton. It was his ambition to be the owner of several banks. When he found the seller of his proposed first bank raising the price at the last minute, he refused to buy at the new price and stayed that night at a small hotel in the town concerned. He got talking to the owner of the hotel who was seeking to sell out. Hilton learned the basics of the hotel business that night, saw the opportunities for profit and bought it. The result of that unexpected failure is the leading hotel in most prestige cities.

When you have an unexpected failure which

forces you to be doing something, going somewhere, saying or thinking something that you wouldn't normally do, ask yourself where the opportunity is. And if you can't see one, ask yourself how you can find it.

Unexpected failure provided opportunity more directly and more embarrassingly for Frank McNamara when he discovered he had no means of payment after dining out in a classy restaurant. It occurred to him that some form of recognized IOU would make dining out easier. That incident was the birth of the credit card generally and Diners Club specifically.

The unexpected failure in your company contains opportunity because it provides you with information you hadn't anticipated or indeed looked for. And further, because the failure occurred within your company, you have total access to all the information associated with it. You don't have this when you are looking at an unexpected failure outside your company.

Find out why the 'whatever' failed. The failure is bristling with information! If you notice anything going unexpectedly wrong in any part of your company, keep a note of it.

Analyse these failures for useful bits of info. Is there a marketing reason for the failure? A production reason? A distribution or any other discernible reason?

War-gaming

Planning or imagining what you would do in the event of various possible war scenarios can generate opportunities. The ideas produced

could range from genuine innovations to simple alterations in operating methods so that you are geared up to cope with various foreseeable crises. The international oil giant, Shell, uses this strategy, and to great effect. Shell staff plan for supply disruption, simulated accidents and disasters on a regular basis. The strategy works so well that when Iraq invaded Kuwait in 1990 (Shell were heavily involved with oil from both), the executive in charge of war-gaming said 'I don't think we missed a beat.' (Van Wacham, 1991). It was business as usual for Shell.

What would you do about supplies and deliveries if some war, political or natural disaster occurred? Thinking along these lines may provide you with better solutions than you currently use. Despite its horrors in reality, war can provide a rich ocean of opportunities through fantasy.

Grow by shrinking

Growing companies often reach a point where future growth is stunted by the sheer size of the organization. Organizations reach a size

which makes them so unresponsive to the market that the best they can hope to do is stagnate for a while before the inevitable decline happens. IBM's dramatic growth, stagnation, then decline with gigantic losses is a case in point.

The best way to counter 'big business blight' is to maintain the small company feeling. Organize the company structure in such a way that it functions like a large number of small businesses pulling in the same direction. Advocates of the economies of scale provided by centralization will say that you'll waste a large amount of resources on duplication in each of the small units. That is true. If the price of flexibility and therefore long-term survival is a little (or even a lot) of tax-allowable duplication, then so be it; it is a price that should be willingly paid. It's no coincidence that some of the most successful business people alive today advocate this policy – including the company that originated JIT (Just In Time – Toyota)). If Richard Branson of Virgin does, and Shoiduro Toyoda of Toyota does, it might be a strategy worth exploring.

How can you grow by shrinking? Which parts of your business would perform better if they were autonomous? How could you give your customers better service by shrinking, or dividing up into smaller more responsive units?

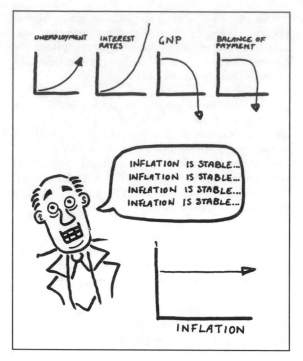

Focus on strength

Solution-led sources of opportunity

- Focus on area of strength
- Opportunity magnetizing
- Unexpected success
- Commoditizing
- Distribution switches
- Objectives focusing
- Overstating objectives
- Working backwards
- The something method
- Wishful thinking
- Designer derivatives
- Quality and other production improvements

Focus on area of strength

Play to your strengths. Politicians often stay in office on the basis of one strength, when everything else is collapsing around them. People don't buy products or services for what they can't do, but for what they can. Nearly every human talent or other asset has a market somewhere. If you focus on the strengths of your company and aim to convert these into a more marketable form, you have found one of the easiest opportunities to identify and exploit. What are your company's key strengths? List them. How do they compare with your competitor's strengths? Which of your strengths are superior to the others? Is your production, marketing, financing, product better in any way? Focus on those and other powers and look for ways to capitalize on these opportunities.

Opportunity magnetizing

Generating publicity as a known winner or achiever will magnetize opportunities to you. There are many users of this strategy; among the most skilful is the Australian, Alan Bond. He realized that the winner's aura would make it easier to attract finance for his various ventures. He set about winning the America's

Cup. Even his first two failed attempts had the desired result.

The media always love a success story. What are you or your staff good at that could generate some publicity? Could you organize an event in your favourite sport or hobby for charity?

Unexpected success

Often a success that comes unexpectedly is either not recognized as a success, or is regarded as a hostile distraction. The reason for this is that you have a focused mind-set of what you think is going to happen, and the unexpected success has no place in that mind-set; it is therefore not regarded as a success. The mental cue to this opportunity is thinking something like: 'That doesn't fit' or 'That shouldn't have happened' or 'I didn't predict this'. To use the strategy, the following rule of thumb will help: When your predictive powers have failed you – don't get defensive: get curious!

The original manufacturers of antibiotics refused to sell them to veterinarians on 'moral' grounds! 'These drugs were developed for humans.' Now a different Swiss company which didn't have any so-called 'moral reasons' for not selling to veterinarians has taken the lead in the world market. The unexpected success that should have been exploited was the realization that vets, too, wanted the drugs. Although this is another example of external unexpected success, the same kind of opportu-

nity can happen internally between departments that serve each other.

As with unexpected failures, keep a note of things that go well, accidental discoveries and so on. In which departments has there been progress that was not anticipated? Have any product-lines suddenly started selling well 'for no apparent reason'? Has any section, department, division out-performed all the others inexplicably? Where have there been positive results that you and your colleagues would not have predicted?

Commoditizing

Spotting or creating a way of giving a large number of people the same needed service has been the making of many industries. Henry Ford 'made' the car industry by mass-producing previously hand-made-to-order products. Various people 'made' the entertainments industry, by building cinemas for mass viewing of one product. If you are providing one product or service, figure out a way in which you could get it to many people. Or if you are providing a range of products or services, how could you standardize one in such a way that customers could benefit from you passing on the reduced costs? 80 per cent of your customers probably buy from only 20 per cent of your products. How can you standardize or mass-produce that 20 per cent to make their price or uniformity more attractive to your customers?

Effectively you can generate opportunity by

Unexpected success

making a premium product/service a commodity or by making a commodity a premium product. In the late 1980s to early 1990s, Dell Computers and several dozen other companies of a similar ilk realized that computers were becoming commodities. Some set up ultra-cheap mail order companies; others set up retail warehouses. IBM failed to realize that their 'premium products' had been commoditized with predictable results.

Focus on a product/service and ask yourself 'How can I commoditize this?'

Distribution switches

Some large businesses function by distributing a product or a service to the customer. Others

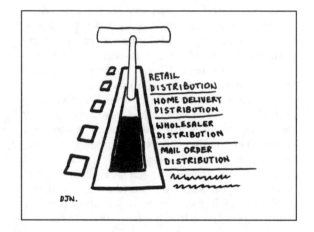

operate on 'arrival distribution' (retail), that is, the customer comes to the business.

Switching between various means of distribution can provide opportunities. The cinema industry is an arrival-based distribution business. When the video recorder was invented and commoditized, various companies set up video rental stores (retail) on the premise that the customer would be prepared to do their own pick-up distribution to control when and where they watched movies. The success of the video rental store concept marked a switch from arrival-based distribution to pick-up or retail distribution.

Then some time later, companies were set up to distribute door-to-door the latest videos for the customers who wanted them but were not prepared to do their own distribution. The success of those companies marked a switch from pick-up, retail distribution to home-delivery distribution.

Many companies have found rich opportunity in doing nothing more innovative than offering an alternative means of distribution to the customer. Of course if you can add something else that the customers want, success is even more likely.

Ikea, the Scandinavian furniture chain, offer low-price high-quality goods to customers who are prepared to pick up their goods from an adjoining warehouse and assemble at home.

What possible ways could you get your customer and product together? Create a list of possible distribution options. Which method are you currently using? What percentage of your possible customers prefer it that way? What ratios of customers would prefer which methods? Are those that wish an expensive means of distribution willing to pay for it? Do some low-cost market research on the alternatives to establish which methods your various types of customers may respond to. Compile a pie chart of preferences and cross-reference those figures with the price tolerance parameters you have established for each segment. Which distribution method would give you the most profitable business? Which would give you the greatest profit/sales ratio?

Objectives focusing

The self-made hyper-rich are widely reported as users of this strategy: 'I decided on my goal and nothing, but nothing was going to stop me!' Adopting that level of intensity and drive will create such determination that you'll find opportunities for achieving your goal. Whereas with a lesser determination, those opportunities might have been invisible to you, or worse still, may have only become visible after the chance had passed. In other words many opportunities become visible at the right time only when you look for them through determined eyes. If you look through negative eyes you see the opportunity, when it's too late, if you see it at all.

For Brian Epstein, the chap who 'made' them, the Beatles became an all-consuming obsession. All those around him regarded his goal as a hopeless task: 'they were scruffy ****s'. But Epstein eventually persuaded them to wear identical suits and trendy hair-styles. He sold them to the world with manic determination.

Be clear about your objective and move heaven and hell to get there! Our objective is to . . . and

OBJECTIVES
OBJECTIVES
OBJECTIVES
OBJECTIVES
OBJECTIVES

Objective focusing

Working backwards

we will achieve it . . . whatever!'

Setting an objective creates opportunities, simply by making you more able to see them. Look at all the objectives your company / department has set. What is your mission statement? What objectives are implicit in that? Examine the ways you plan to achieve your objectives. Can they be achieved in other ways? Need some of them be achieved at all? What is the level of commitment to achieving the objectives? Would some other way of achieving the objective create a higher level of commitment? What methods can you use to create maximum commitment in those charged with achieving?

Overstated objectives

A variant of the above. By outlandishly exaggerating your objectives you may spark some useful ideas. First list the component elements of your objective, then exaggerate each. Then ask yourself how you could achieve the new sub-goals. In what ways would the original goal be enhanced by the new higher level sub-goals?

Working backwards

Take some internal objective you have, define your desired end-state specifically and exactly (as opposed to characteristically as in the Something method). Then work backwards, looking for potential solutions that will take you to the end-state.

It is speculated that the famous 'bouncing bomb' was invented using this method. Speculating about what empowering question was asked might lead to: 'How can we attack a target with a bomb travelling horizontally as opposed to vertically?' You can see that the desired end-state is defined exactly: a horizontally travelling bomb.

Work backwards from the very specifically defined end-state. Ask questions which may be phrased like: How can we achieve . . .? How many different ways could we achieve . . .? What solution(s) will take me to . . . position? Having come up with some solution(s), ask similar questions about getting to that point. Work all the way back until you have a conventional MBO (management by objectives) sequence to achieve your goal.

The something method

As stated before, except that you apply the strategy to an internal concept in your search for opportunity. 'I want SOMETHING that will cut down our . . . overheads.' 'I want something to increase our . . .' The opportunities are found by asking deliberately vague questions as opposed to the more conventional approach which is to impose preconceived solution ideas on the problem. To use the strategy, you define the characteristics of some end point you'd like to reach but sufficiently vaguely so that several things could satisfy them.

Wishful thinking

'I wish we could . . .' Einstein contended that imagination was more powerful than intellect. Given that his mathematical education was to

55

Wishful thinking

aesthetics, environmental friendliness . . .

Design can radically change the market performance of a product. Black and Decker's hand-held vacuum cleaner was experiencing slumping sales. The designers were let loose. The results were most impressive and getting better. I had to fight hard to not say the results were a clean sweep. Oops, too late. Other companies base the bulk of their marketing and production strategies on the designer image of their product, with great success. Reebok, for instance.

The best commercial design is that which is in tune with contemporary images and symbolism. There is a strong link between design and trends, fads and so on. You can strengthen this strategy by using it in conjunction with the Trends, Fads and Symbolism strategies.

What percentage of your revenues goes on design (above and beyond functional design)? What percentage of your development costs

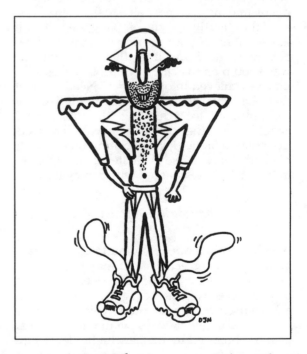

goes on design? What is your annual spend on design update as a percentage of each product's sales?

say the least 'lacking' when he formulated his theories, one can only assume that imagination was what led to his discoveries. In fact, we know that he imagined what would be seen sitting on the tip of a beam of light.

Fantasize. What outlandish objectives would you like to achieve? Don't edit what you come up with and don't avoid going down some fantasy roads because you think the path they take is too unrealistic. In fact the more unrealistic you are, the more creative you'll probably be. What would be so unbelievably good that you almost couldn't believe it if you achieved it? What achievement would your friends not believe if you told them about it? Now use that fantasy objective as your starting point and use some of the other stratagems above, or your normal management thinking to take your fantasy into the realms where it could become a possibility. See also Overstated objectives.

Devise a designer derivative

Some companies have found enormous opportunities for increased sales simply by taking a very ordinary product and giving it visual appeal. The 'designer' added-value products sell better than their plain competitors. Particularly if they are similarly priced. Good design can address your customers' every need: functionality, how it feels, ease of repair,

Quality and other production improvements

This is a specific version of objectives focusing, but it is less definitive and at the same time it is

Quality improvements

never achievable; it is ongoing. Since there is much written about this and many companies already pursue 'quality' as a formal policy, there will be no teaching granny to suck eggs.

TQM (Total Quality Management) and quality circles, although not new ideas, do give a starting or focus point from which to look for opportunities. Could you introduce JIT (Just In Time) or MRPII (Manufacturing Resource Planning) or your own internalized version of them? Which departments might benefit (it needn't be production only)? Would going for BS 5750 (UK only), or ISO 9000 validation help you focus more clearly? Or enable you to gain wider cooperation in your search for opportunities? Could you make quality control a first

step toward introducing an opportunity culture?

Reminder exercise: Have you remembered to devise at least two empowering questions for each strategy presented?

Exercise: You have now examined both internal and external opportunity source strategies. Which of the strategies are similar? Which of the internal strategies could be, or even ought to be, external strategies, and vice versa?

Exercise: Ask the questions necessary to convert any strategy to the opposite category.

Exercise: Which observation strategies could be/ought to be problem-led or solution-led? Which solution-led strategy ought to be . . .? Which problem-led could be . . .? What questions could you ask to change a problem-led strategy into a solution-led one? Or an observation-led strategy? Or any combination of change you can think of?

Exercise: What order and categories would you have organized the strategies in?

Exercise: What could be gained from putting each strategy on a single card?

3

Psychological Strategies

The strategies described below are psychological methods known to be useful during the creative process. Some can be used independently, others can best be used in conjunction with another strategy. These strategies are less dependent on gathered information than the external and internal opportunity source strategies.

- Moving epicentres
- Creative ignorance
- Inner dialogue control
- Creative alarm clock
- Yes, but . . .
- But/and exchange
- Synonym/Antonym
- Functional fluidity
- Constraint analysis
- Build on ideas
- Build in ideas
- Be outrageous/role play
- Word association
- Stimulate a sentence
- Analogize
- Analogy association
- Metaphorize and metaphor association
- Ask Anna for an anaphor analysis
- Action phrase it
- Name it now, invent it later
- Dream strategies

Moving epicentres

Moving epicentres is best for organizing your thinking prior to starting the idea hunt. Take the central point in whatever area you are seeking ideas. Write the word or short phrase in small but legible writing in the centre of a large sheet of paper. Put a circle round it. Ask

participants for ideas closely related to the main points and write them, inside small circles, so that they surround the original circle or epicentre. Take each of these second generation ideas and write them round a concentric circle some distance from the centre, sufficiently well-spaced around the circumference so that each can form its own epicentre when it has its own satellite points added. Repeat the process until the page is full. Using different coloured pens will make the flow of ideas easier to follow. You can vary the criterion for adding satellites to any point. Carry out the exercise with a different criterion each time. To be optimally creative in using the method, have no criteria or rules to say what is and what is not a related point. When completed, start asking empowering questions, about the relationships between ideas, for instance.

Creative ignorance

A publicly stated strategy of Clive Sinclair is that if he wants to learn about a subject, he'll get hold of the simplest possible book ('An idiot's guide to . . .'), learn the basics and do his own thinking from then on. What does that strategy offer? It's more a case of what it leaves out: if you don't know a subject area, you don't know what can't be done. You are unconstrained by lack of knowledge, and will be completely ignorant of how creative what you suggest is.

When a whole gaggle of academics were proving flight was impossible, the Wright brothers were out there doing it! A flock of similar ilk were 'proving' human-powered flight was not possible when the Gossamer Albatross was flying over the English Channel and the Icarus project was cruising a few feet above the Mediterranean Sea.

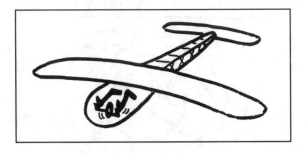

Creative ignorance

King C. Gillette was told by the 'experts' of his day that he would never get a shaving edge on thin sheet steel. Of that mentality he said 'If I had been technically trained, I would probably have given up or probably would never have begun. But', and here is the key, 'But, I didn't know enough to quit.'

Huge Heffner said after setting up the huge international success, *Playboy*, 'The only reason I tried it was that I had no conception of the almost insurmountable difficulties and the odds against my success. If I had known what I know now, I doubt if I would have even tried.' In instances like these 'ignorance is power'.

There are several ways you can capitalize on creative ignorance: whom do you know who knows nothing about the field in which you want to look for an opportunity? Ask them what they think. Give them the basics; don't mention any of the problems and don't set any constraints.

Occasionally you will not have to ask for an 'ignorant opinion'. A father while taking his daughter's photograph was asked when she could see the pictures. As he was explaining that it took time, it occurred to him that people all over the world would like instant photography. Edwin Land then had the motive and direction to invent the Polaroid camera.

Reverse the situation – which fields do you know little or nothing about? Perhaps looking there for an opportunity might prove useful! You could look at the problems and see if your ignorance enables you to come up with a solution which the informed cannot. Remember to phrase your questions in a positive way. You could combine this strategy with Role playing (see later) by role playing someone you know would be ignorant of the area in which you are seeking solutions or opportunities.

Exercise: Devise two other ways in which you could use this strategy in your company.

Inner dialogue control

The strongest piece of evidence I have ever come across to support the notion that what you think will determine the results you get is the Roger Bannister example. If Roger Bannister had told himself that the 4-minute mile couldn't be broken, do you think he'd have broken it? If you tell yourself that an idea has potential and that it will be worth exploring further – will it have?

Your inner dialogue is entirely within your control. What you choose to think will determine how you feel, which will in turn determine how you behave, which in turn will determine what results you achieve. If you make empowering statements or ask yourself empowering questions with your inner dialogue, you probably won't be surprised to know that the likelihood of positive results is enormously increased.

The inner dialogue and, hence, performance of other runners was significantly changed by knowledge of Roger Bannister's achievement. Within two years of his under 4-minute mile, 30 (plus) other runners had done the same!

Examples of empowering dialogues: 'That's an interesting idea'; 'I'm sure we could take that

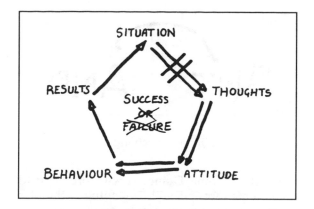

Inner dialogue control: the pentagon principle

Creative alarm clock

further'; 'There's bound to be something positive in that'; 'Good starting point; now how can I build on it?'

What kinds of positive empowering statements and questions should you be subvocalizing to enhance your Opportunity-Spotting chances? Compile a list of empowering questions that could be applied to any idea. Do you think it would be a good idea to compile a list of positive and empowering inner dialogue statements which you can use to counter the effects of doubt and negativity entering your mind?

Exercise: Compile a list of empowering questions and statements that you will use as an aid to Opportunity-Spotting.

Creative alarm clock

How frequently have you found you can come up with a solution just in time to beat an important deadline? What seems to happen is that your mind registers the deadline, quietly gathers information, and generates a solution in line with your motivation level. Many people seem to use this as a strategy, often unwittingly. You can harness this phenomenon by choosing when you want an answer to your question. Top-level athletes consistently manage to get themselves in peak condition just at the right time.

Take your problem in your mind and decide that you will have a solution by such and such a date at a specific time. Before setting the alarm clock, thoroughly go over the problem; understand all the angles and ramifications, then ask your mind to solve the problem for you. Then forget about it until the required

date. If you get an idea in the meantime, note it down with the rest of the information and forget about it again. You could set your creative alarm clock to make you feel creative at a certain time, for instance to be creative at your next opportunity-creation meeting.

Exercise: In what other ways could you use the creative alarm clock strategy? In what ways do you think you could enhance and maximize its effects?

Yes, but . . .

Often ideas are criticized by a sentence which starts 'Yes, but . . .' Strangely, although 'Yes, but . . .' is meant as a diplomatic put-down of the idea the 'but' part of the sentence may contain opportunity ideas. The speaker may have unwittingly put his or her finger on the opportunity button. 'Yes, but . . .' usually indicates that the person concerned can see the opportunity, but feels the 'but' represents an insurmountable obstacle and as such the idea ought to be dropped.

The idea may be 95 per cent achievable, with the obstacle representing the small, 5 per cent, but insurmountable barrier. If you thought all you had to do to have a great opportunity is overcome the 5 per cent barrier, that is where

Yes, but . . .

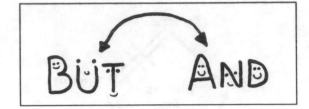

But/and exchange

make it coherent. Doing so will force you to consider more possible meanings, thereby increasing your chances of being creative.

The objective of this strategy is to help you see opportunity where you'd intended to make an excuse for not seeing it. If you hear yourself or others making excuses why something can't be done, swap the 'ands' and the 'buts' around.

Synonym/antonym strategy

In the same way that you can change the meaning of a sentence by swapping the 'buts' and 'ands', you can do so with any pair of antonyms. You could swap the 'can'ts' for 'cans', impossible for possible . . . The strategy will probably work best in a group where each member can immediately change any negative word for its positive opposite.

Most words are not at the extremes of whatever dimension they sit on. Some words are more positive than others. You can make statements more empowering by replacing slightly positive words with their extremely positive synonyms. For example, 'this might be a good idea' would become 'this is a great idea'. You are more likely to put some serious effort into a great idea than you would into a 'might be' idea. And if you think in more empowered ways, you are more likely to obtain results (see Inner dialogue control).

Exercise: Compile a vertical list of well-known excuse words on the left-hand side of a page, and on the right-hand side write the opposite. Use the list when using this strategy.

Exercise: Compile a list of more positive synonyms to commonly used, slightly positive words.

you would direct your efforts, wouldn't you? So, when you hear 'Yes, but', you know all that stands between you and an opportunity is the barrier you've just been told about.

Exercise: What ideas have you recently discarded by 'Yes, butting' them? Reconsider the ideas; how can you overcome those barriers?

But/and exchange

This strategy is similar to 'Yes, but', but it can be used with any sentence structure. When people make excuses about why something can't be done, they invariably use the words 'and' and 'but'. The whole meaning of what they/you say can be changed if you swap the 'ands' and 'buts'. The meaning can change from one indicating problem to one indicating opportunity. For example, 'I want to look for opportunities but 'I've no staff with Opportunity -Spotting skills'.

Changing the 'but' for an 'and' makes the statement sound less like a reason for not Opportunity Spotting. 'I want to look for opportunities AND I've no staff with Op-Spot skills' sounds like a cue to train the staff or find an Op-Spotting strategy that doesn't depend on staff skills. Often when you exchange 'and' and 'but', the new sentence will make no sense at all. That may appear to undermine the strategy.

Not so! If the new sentence is nonsense, you'll have to consider altering it in some way to

Functional fluidity

The process of trying to imagine what something could be in an alternative guise enables you to get out of thinking in a fixed way about whatever that thing is. It's almost as though you've given yourself permission to break your own rules about that something. Breaking rules seems to be a major ingredient in creativity. Don't be afraid to break a few. Indeed it would help if you actively sought to shatter as many rules as possible.

Take a problem, a concept, an anything and answer the question: 'What else could this be?' It may help to try to express the object under consideration pictorially to give your thinking another dimension. You could use the strategy in a compound way by asking the question of the last answer given rather than the original concept. Using the strategy in a compound way will (like the following strategy) help you to uncover, alter or drop the epistemes (unstated but commonly held rules or assumptions).

Exercise: Generate five responses to the question, 'what else could this book be?' Please, be

What else could it be?

polite!

Constraint analysis

Have you ever tried to solve a puzzle, failed, been told the obvious answer and been furious? Yes? You feel cheated somehow. You feel the puzzle-setter implied that you could only solve it in one of a few ways and then moved the goalposts? Had you known *that* was OK, you'd have solved it yourself. Right? In effect you had bound yourself with assumed or imagined rules and constraints.

When trying to solve a problem, analyse and try to verbalize the constraints that bind you. Understanding what rules are applied to a particular problem can help you re-define how you could solve it. The constraints can be real or imagined, flexible or rigid or in some cases non-existent.

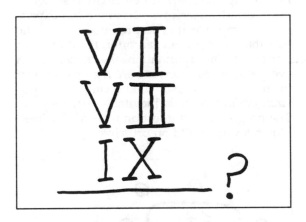

Constraint analysis

Solve the problem in the Figure by converting the 9 into a 6 with one stroke of your pen.

The constraint that could stop you solving the IX problem is that there is an expectation that the solution is Roman numerals based. As soon as you identify and understand that constraint and challenge its validity, you can solve the problem.

Start with a problem. What assumptions do you have about the rules you have to follow to solve the problem. Define and identify the constraints on you. Which constraints are real? Which are imaginary? Having identified the imaginary constraints, have another bash at the problem. Of the real constraints, are there any ways you can fulfil them by being 'liberal with the rules'? Doing this exercise in a group will give a broader view of the constraints. The process of uncovering the constraints will guide you towards the solution. Indeed, in many cases, the constraints may define the characteristics of the solution.

Exercise: Join up the dots without taking your pen off the page and in no more than four straight lines:

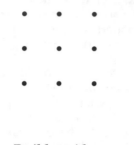

Build on ideas

Frequently, the spark for creativity is someone else's idea to which we can apply our experience to improve it. The provided idea is the best the other person can offer. If we can add our best to that foundation, the chances of an even better idea emerging are high. Most great inventors and artists unknowingly use this strategy; indeed it is inevitable that they do. The progression of addition tools for business illustrates the 'build on principle'.

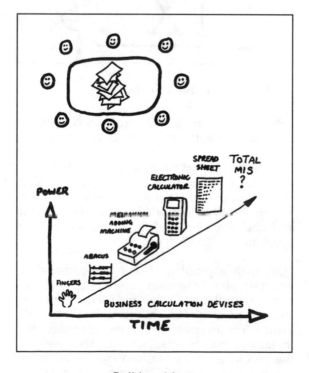

Build on ideas

This strategy is best used in a group. Everyone in the group is to write some idea about an agreed problem on a sheet of paper, one idea per sheet, on as many sheets as you can come up with ideas, perhaps using other strategies. Put your sheets in a pile at the centre of the table as you go along. When you are exhausted of ideas, take an idea sheet (not one of your own) and see how you can build on it, improve on it, modify it, make it simpler, more marketable, easier to use, better for . . ., widen its use (make it more generalized), make it highly specific in its use, see what other possible or even probable uses it could have . . . When you are exhausted on that idea, put the sheet back in the pile and pick another one (take the first that is available: being choosy will be counter-productive) and carry on the process for no more than 40 minutes.

Gather together all the ideas and record them on some centrally visible medium (flipchart, wall-sized whiteboard, and so on). One idea should be read out at a time, with a different person for each idea. This will give everyone else a chance to make additions and suggestions for improvements. Do not allow any criticial judgements at this stage. This method can also be used in the enhancement of ideas.

Build in ideas

Similar to Build on ideas. Take a pile of generated ideas and build them into each other to create new combined ideas.

1 One person selects two cards at random from a pile of ideas (put each idea on a card).
2 The whole team tries to find a way/ways to build the ideas into each other.

Exercise: In what ways could you build this strategy in to others?

Be outrageous – role play

Many psychological studies have found that if you role play being creative, you'll be more creative than you would be otherwise. It seems that the more outrageous the role you play, the more creative you'll be!

Imagine yourself as a way-out creative, Bohemian type. Look at the problem or a field of opportunity you have chosen to explore and

Left brain thinking –
  Logical/Analytical/Verbal
Right brain thinking –
  Emotional/Intuitive
Rear brain thinking –
  Visual/Pictorial
Front brain thinking –
  Self-control/Inhibition
Deep mid-brain thinking –
  Basic life functions 'thinking'
Whole brain thinking –
  Aesthetic/Well-being

be as outrageous as possible with your suggestions.

Put yourself right in the shoes (if s/he has any!) of this far-out character and imagine what they would suggest.

You can widen your role playing way beyond being merely Bohemian. In fact any human characteristic you care to mention can be role played and aid your creativity level. You might imagine that role playing characteristics you have yourself won't lead to creativity. Not so. We are all complex creatures with many facets to our personalities. We can't show all our facets at the same time. But by systematically role playing as many parts of ourselves as possible we can access the creativity potential inherent in each. We think in many different ways too, but not all at the same time. Create a list of the ways in which you think. And role play thinking in those styles. So, if I was doing this exercise I'd list:

Then I'd systematically apply or role play each of the above kinds of thinking to the problem or opportunity area.

Create a list of all the ways in which people act or behave. Role play solving your problem or searching for opportunities while behaving, or acting as though you are behaving, in one of your listed ways.

Create a list of all the ways people feel and . . . as above.

Since all possible human activity can be explained in terms of thinking, feeling or behaving, and as there seems to be an infinite variety of each, you should never run out of roles to play. Potentially creative roles can be found in many places; use your thesaurus to generate roles, particularly from words that describe thinking, feeling, or behaviour; you could also use your observations of bizarre people in the course of your life, using some of these as the basis for role playing. Perhaps you could go as far as using an appropriate character to generate more characters.

Exercise: Devise or perhaps even draw a series of outrageous characters to use as vehicles for this strategy.

Word association

Often having thought of one word, it's near impossible not to come up with a connected word. The connection can be of any type: sound, meaning, context . . . The key point is that by word-associating you allow yourself to make seemingly illogical links. After and only after you've made those links, you can look to see if there is any meaning or benefit that can be exploited.

There are at least three ways you can use this strategy:

Be outrageous

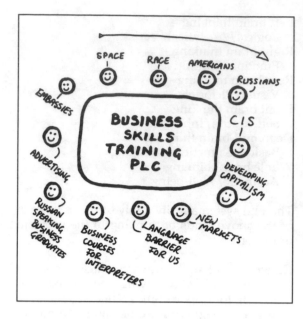

Word association

1 Random Word Association (RWA)
2 Focused Word Association (FWA)
3 Attribute Word Association (AWA)

All are best carried out in a group. Using RWA, start with a word at random. Leave the selection of the word up to the first person in the group. Whichever word they generate is the cue for the next person to come up with the first word that comes to mind.

One person should be uninvolved and logging the responses for consideration later. Go through all the words and try to establish what prompted them. This will give you some idea pointers. The link between each word (as explained by the person who came up with the new word) is more informative and laden with ideas than the word itself.

Ask empowering questions about the links. What opportunities can you see in the links? What unusual angle does it suggest? Sometimes (frequently?) there will be no mileage in a particular link. In that case take a sequence of two, three, four or more links, and ask yourself where the sequence is pointing to. Where could it end up?

With FWA, the same as above applies but you start with a word strongly linked to the opportunity field you are examining and each subsequent word must be linked in some way to that area.

A more specific version of the FWA strategy is Attribute Word Association (AWA) in which words that describe characteristics of the focus area are the preferred link. Although in the absence of the generation of a relevant attribute, the first thing that comes to mind is preferable to keep the creative flow going. The end result is used in the same way as RWA.

Word shapes

Prepare a list of attributes that best describe the focus area. Place the words in a shape that corresponds to their number, that is, place three words in a triangle on a sheet of paper, four in a square, five in a . . . and so on.

Put the words together by linking the points of whatever shape was created. List all the possible combinations of words, but more importantly list the new ways that they make you think of the problem or opportunity area. As usual, ask empowering questions about the unusual combinations of words that are created.

Stimulate a sentence

You've probably noticed that sometimes you start a sentence without quite knowing what you intend to say, or more likely how you intend to say what you want to. You might also have found yourself half-way through a sentence in such a position that the only way to complete the sentence in a grammatically correct way is to make it up as you go along. I've

done this and been embarrassed, but I've also done it and found myself breaking new intellectual ground. In short, digging yourself out of a grammatical hole can spark creativity.

Prepare a list of words that define a problem or opportunity area. Randomly arrange the words (perhaps by putting each one on a card and shuffling the pack). Deal the cards and note the order. Get everyone in the group to make a sentence from the words, keeping the order as dealt. It would be preferable to do this verbally and spontaneously. Note down each person's version of the sentence. And, more importantly, the ideas it sparks. Ask empowering questions about the sentences generated. And of the ideas generated.

Repeat the process with a different order of words. You could enhance the spontaneity of the process by making the sentence up as each card is dealt.

Analogize

Creating an analogy for the problem you are addressing, or an opportunity you are seeking, enables you to think about it in a more detached and dispassionate way. The invention of the sewing machine came from a dream in which the inventor was being poked at by tribal warriors with holes in the end of their

Analogize

spears. Creating an analogy also gives you licence to be outrageous and worse! (Or rather, better in terms of creativity!)

Outline a problem that you feel is opportunity-rich. Ask everyone involved to put forward analogies. Which problem is this problem like? Can you think of related or parallel problems? Then gather together all the analogies, pick one and devise a solution to that analogous problem. Pick another, and so on. Now try to apply those solutions to your original problem.

An example: A cash flow problem may be seen as a bottomless pit down which money disappears. What would you do? Cork the pit! How does that transfer to a cash flow problem? How about stopping all outgoing payments for a week?

Exercise: Compile a list of problem analogies as illustrative examples to your group.

Analogy association

In the same way that words cue other words in your mind, analogies cue other analogies. Create a list of the attributes associated with a problem or opportunity area you are examining. Create an analogy, then use it or the list of attributes to spark another analogy. And so on until you have a list of analogies. Examine the list, and ask the originator of each analogy what sparked the idea. Even if the person concerned cannot explain the spark, ask them to find some meaning. Encourage others to offer their theories too. Ask empowering questions about whatever answers are given. How can we use that? In what way could we incorporate that into . . .? Like its word-based relative, the analogy association method can be random, focused, or attribute-based.

Metaphorize

'I want this computer to be equipped like a 747.' 'He/she is a lion/ess in the boardroom.' 'It's the Rolls-Royce of widgets.' You can use this strategy in three ways.

1 See the similarity between two elements first and then create the metaphor. By creating a metaphor for something, you see it from a slightly different perspective. Ask empowering questions about these different perspectives.

2 Being even more creative you can reverse

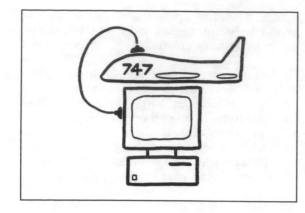

Metaphorize

the process: choose or even devise a metaphor and look for ways it can be related to your opportunity area; find out what it generates in the mind of others. Ask them to justify how the metaphor is linked to your opportunity area.

3 Create a list of metaphors from metaphor association in the same way you would create a list of words from word association, or analogies from analogy association. The metaphor associations can be random, focused, or attribute determined. Or indeed any other association you care to devise.

In practice a metaphorizing session might go like this: get each member of the group to suggest a metaphor for the problem or opportunity area. For instance you might be looking at your debtor days problem and suggest 'You need to collect debts like a bee collects pollen'. That leads one to think that since the bee is collecting for its own as well as its hive's purposes and therefore puts a lot of energy into it, that you could be more effective if some commission scheme were implemented for your debt recovery department. The key here is to suggest the metaphor first before analysing it. Suggest any metaphor; it doesn't have to make sense.

Exercise: Compile a list of example metaphors for the purposes of illustrating the strategy to your staff.

Ask Anna for an anaphor analysis

The principle behind this strategy is to use the ambiguity of, imprecision in, and the need to read between the lines of, language to create ideas.

Anna went for a run and Bill did too.

You know what that sentence means from a first reading, but how did you know? You knew from the anaphor. That is, from the second part of the sentence 'Bill did too' which alludes to the fact, or somehow implies, that Bill went for a run. Does it also imply that Bill went for a run with Anna? Some will say yes, some will say no. All, I hope, will recognize that the possible different interpretations could cue opportunity thinking.

Generate a list of words associated with your product or service. Use adjectives, nouns, any word that could be even loosely associated. Use the words as the raw material for the group to generate a series of anaphors. The second sentence in the anaphor draws the bulk of its meaning from the meaning contained in the first, but the relationship need not be an 'also' or a 'too' although I will stick to those relationships for the purposes of simplicity. Here are some examples of generated anaphors with a way of handling them:

1 Microwaves change the temperature of food, so do fridges.
2 Microwaves transmit energy. Fridges do likewise.
3 Microwaves are all around us. So are fridges.
4 Microwaves are just one part of a larger spectrum. So are fridges.

The meaning focus (MF) and possible opportunities of each anaphor are:

1 MF: temperature change. Ideas – cooling by microwave?
2 MF: ambiguous – temp change or communication? Ideas – what communication possibilities are there in a fridge? Freezer temp warning signal? Fridge section warning signal (not cool enough – possible food poisoning)? Hygiene – 'smell detector' warning signal?
3 MF: Frequency omnipresence – appliance omnipresence ambiguity. Idea – must be some electromagnetic phenomenon that has cooling effect!
4 MF: product range – frequency range ambiguity. Idea – expand range of fridges? We have combined grill/microwave, so what advantages would there be in a combined fridge/microwave?

There is a second way to use anaphors. Highly intelligent people often generate 'near anaphors' by accident. They utter two sentences, the second of which appears to be unrelated to the first. In the mind of the speaker, several other thoughts have been uttered in the short space of time between the verbalization of the spoken thoughts. To the genius and the speaker, the two sentences follow. For the rest of us, speculating as to what wonderful inventions, opportunities or ideas could link the two sentences is the best we can hope for.

Take a note of the near anaphors you hear and generate ideas from attempting to make sense of them.

You could use the above method in a more controlled way. Ask each member of a group to write on a card one short sentence about anything they wish or related in some way to the problem or opportunity field you are considering. Gather the cards, shuffle them, and deal out two at a time. Treat them as being anaphorically connected and try to explain how one leads to the other or how the second draws part of its meaning from the first.

Action phrase it

Many business problems are abstract. Ideas that we generate in the search for opportunities are often abstract. If you impose concrete real-world actions on the concepts, you can find new ways of looking at them, or perhaps even change your perceptions. If you say of an abstract concept 'make it bigger' what happens? Make God bigger. What happens? Probably your mind will fill with all sorts of

interesting possibilities. Mix the abstract with the concrete, the inactive with the active.

Creativity can be sparked by bringing together concepts that normally don't come together or better still by bringing together concepts that clash!

Ask everyone in the group to write down 10 to 15 'action phrases'. An action phrase is any statement that will change the problem or might alter the opportunity, for example make it wider, buy it cheaper, market it faster, make it green, store it, beautify it, and so on. Apply several action words or combinations of action words to one concept. Collect all the ideas and consider them, or treat the ideas to a little more creativity before you evaluate them.

Name it now, invent it later

Kids are very creative when they are learning language. They make words up and judge whether they fit the rules. You can harness this innate tendency by:

1   Creating a list of weird names and words, and
2   Inventing products, services or improvements to fit the names.

For those who find being weird rather difficult, use names and words associated with your industry. Randomly combine them, perhaps by putting the words on cards, then shuffle

Action phrase it

and deal them in pairs. Note the descriptive name formed by each pair on a list. Finish dealing and start inventing.

Dream strategies

Dreaming is a part of intellectual life that is ignored by many, particularly those of an analytical disposition. Creative types have known throughout the centuries that dreams can produce some real gems. Paul McCartney has attributed the writing of some of his songs to having woken up with the completed song in his head. Many other artists have made similar attributions. Lorenzo's father (of Lorenzo's Oil fame) was reported as having come up with the basis for treatment of the disease ALD in a dream. You've probably solved at least one or two problems in your dreams, or know someone who has. Recent research has shown that we can alter the course of our dreams, and even programme ourselves to dream about a particular subject.

To harness this power you can use either or both of the following.

Dream alteration

The next time you become aware that you are dreaming, decide to alter the course of your dream, just to prove to yourself that you can do it. The following night, decide before going to

bed what problem or opportunity area you are going to incorporate in the dream. When you realize you are dreaming, inject the topics you wish. You will quickly realize that the dream will start taking its own direction again after a short while. The following evening, having proven that you can introduce whatever subject you wish, experiment with keeping the dream on track, perhaps by re-introducing your topic or by introducing it in a different way. You are now ready to use your dreams as an opportunity resource.

Dream programming

To some extent you will need to have experience of dream alteration to maximize your chances of successful dream programming. Simply decide that when you dream, you are going to dream about successfully spotting, seeking or creating opportunities. To programme your mind, picture yourself in the search, visualize yourself asking empowering questions in the dream, then picture yourself reacting to finding a suitable opportunity.

For both strategies it is probably wise to keep a pen and paper by your bed. When you get an idea, you must wake yourself from the dream and write it down; you will almost certainly forget the idea if you don't. Most people's memory of their dreams is poor. Some have crystal-clear dream memories, but until you know which you are, you ought to assume you'll forget your brilliant ideas if you don't write them down. Happy dreaming!

Summary note on maximizing your methods

Whereas the internal and external opportunity source methods can only be used by those with specific information, the psychological strategies are not dependent on detailed information. They can be used by anyone. However, that is not to say that the psychological strategies need be kept clear of information. Quite the contrary; if you can combine them with the power contained in commercial information the effect will be like turbocharging a car.

Exercise: Go through each of the psychological strategies and decide what kinds of information could make them more powerful.

Exercise: Which of the psychological strategies could be combined with which internal or external strategies to produce some seriously powerful hybrids?

Exercise: Now that you have completed all the exercises, devise an overall structure with which you will apply the new information to your company/department/section.

Exercise: Go through the strategies you've just read about and use them to come up with at least six ideas. It's important that you do this; we'll need the ideas to work on in the next section.

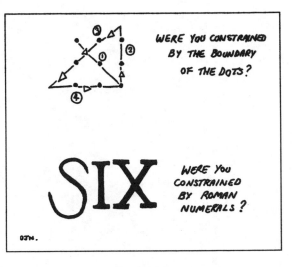

Puzzle answers

4

Enhancing opportunities

Introduction

The ideas you have generated are the raw material of opportunity. You will probably feel they are rough, crass or even incomplete. As potential opportunities they probably are. They will become actual opportunities only after you have processed and added value to them. The process of enhancing ideas will move them away from the abstract and conceptual towards the more functional and practical end of the creative spectrum.

Keep in mind that you should still not be judging any ideas at this stage; you will do that in the evaluation phase of the process. Generating and enhancing great ideas must be separate from the judging process. Creativity is least inhibited when the evaluation of ideas is done at a separate time. The more distant the judging process is from the creative process, the more creative you'll be. Enhancing ideas further before judging them will mean the ideas will probably reach a higher level of 'usability' and you will have a greater sense of their worth before judging.

Exercise: What other advantages could there be to this multi-staged process of Op-Spotting? How can you use it in your company?

Some of the methods below won't apply to many ideas. The best way to use enhancement methods is to run your idea past each one and see if it can be applied. If so, use it. If not, go on to the next technique.

A few of the enhancement strategies will bear a strong resemblance to the original idea-generation methods. Indeed, many of the spotting methods can be used as enhancing methods with only minor, if any, alterations. Some can even be seen as dual-purpose. The obvious dual-purpose methods will be listed again in this section with a brief, often single question, guide to how to use it as an opportunity-enhancement strategy. You may wish to go further and run your ideas past all the spotting methods as a means of finding even more enhancement methods.

Exercise: Read through the enhancement section at least once before running ideas past the various methods presented.

The enhancement of ideas

- Category chameleons
- Tailor the idea
- Similar to . . . ideas
- Opposite angle enhancement
- Different from . . . ideas
- Functional fluidity
- Designer derivative
- Isolation of the key principle
- Focus on area of strength
- Build on it
- Action phrase it
- The AID method: Advantages/Interesting/Disadvantages
- Focus on weakness and Tao tactics
- Disadvantage into advantage
- Lily pads
- Moving epicentres
- The UFP method: Uniqueness/Functionality/Pluses

- Wishful thinking and creative ignorance
- Spell it out
- Build in ideas, symbiosis and partnership
- Network knitting, piggybacking and tap into . . .
- Information available/required
- Working backwards and the something method
- Convince/satisfy/share the background assumptions with me
- Define for me

Category chameleons

When you come to enhance your ideas, the chances are that you'll have several. We know from learning-performance studies that you can widen and deepen your understanding of

information and of your ideas by organizing them into categories. First into two categories, then reorganize into three categories, then four, and so on until each idea falls into its own category. Then change to completely different category headings and do the same again. Your perceptions of the ideas will be changed and enhanced like a chameleon changing colour as it moves over different backgrounds.

Exercise: Compile a list of generic headings which you can use to categorize your ideas. Add to, update and modify this list on a regular basis to avoid your thinking becoming stale.

Tailor the idea

Alter the idea to make it fit the business or situation you are in. This method, like most of the

Tailor the idea

other enhancement methods, stops you from immediately dumping the idea and encourages you to seek ways in which the idea can be altered rather than rejected.

Perhaps the ill-fated C5 might have been successful had it been fitted with a suit. Probably not, but tailoring the C5 will give you a vivid image with which to remember this strategy.

Is there any way the idea can be made to measure? So the idea isn't quite right: how can you alter it? Downscale it? Apply it to a different department? Maybe it will work with a different product? Perhaps combine it with that idea we discarded last week?

Similar to . . . ideas

Ideas that are similar to others are in danger of being like the baby thrown out with the bathwater. Probably the most natural response to, and the most commonly used 'terminator' of, similar ideas is: 'That's the same as . . . that old idea' implying that because the idea is the same as something else, it cannot be innovative and therefore has nothing new to offer. The most constructive way to cope with such a response is to encourage a look beyond the similarities with something like 'It may be, but let's look at the differences to see if we can develop a new idea from them'. It may also be useful to point out to anyone damning an idea that using this 'terminator phrase' is like saying 'The wheel is the same as the rocket; it merely gets you from A to B'!

Bridge A is similar to Bridge B. The difference is that Bridge B has a curved construction. We now know that curved constructions of this

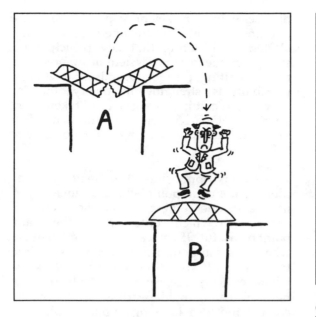

Similar to . . . ideas

type are stronger than those of type A.

Focus on the differences – that is where the opportunity information is. Look for differences across various dimensions. How is it different? What are the differences in terms of functionality? Are there any production differences? What would be the marketing differences? How does it vary in terms of attractiveness, in terms of . . ., and so on?

Exercise: Compile a list of general questions aimed at highlighting the differences between any two ideas that may be accused of being similar.

Opposite angle enhancement

Enhance ideas by looking at the opposite area to that to which the idea applies. A marketing idea (information provision) could be enhanced by looking for ways in which information seeking could help (marketing research?). An accounting idea (event record-keeping) could be enhanced by examining how the related events occur (event generation). What is the conceptual opposite of your idea? How could that area help?

Different from . . . ideas

When an idea strikes you as being different from . . . or not quite what you were looking for, the most informative place to focus will be

on the similarities. 'Different ideas' can often be dismissed as being 'too radical', 'ahead of its time' and so on. While those criticisms may be true, there is usually some potential to be exploited from the idea. The potential strength of a 'different' idea is sometimes in the way it can provide the same benefits as other established products or services, but in a slightly different way.

For example, a wind turbine is different from an oil-fired power station. The instructive similarity is they can both produce electricity. The opportunity lies in the fact that they do the

Different from . . . ideas

same thing in different circumstances. When there is wind, you have cheap electricity from the turbines; when there is none, the power stations can be used.

To use this treatment method, focus on the similarities – they are informative. Ask yourself such questions as:

> Across what dimensions is it similar, in size, in value . . .?
> What similar benefits could/does it provide?

Exercise: Draw up a list of questions aimed at highlighting the similarities between any two ideas.

Functional fluidity

What else could it (the idea) be? What other uses besides that for which it was devised could it have?

Designer derivative

How can the idea be given 'designer appeal'?

Isolation of the key principle

Every idea (here we are referring to ideas you have generated to create opportunities) has one key principle behind it. Once isolated, the key principle can be worked on, improved and so on without the restrictions that its context (or supporting principles) may have imposed on it. As an alternative to modifying the key point, it may be useful to keep the point and change the contexts: if it is no use in one context, it may be useful in another.

As an example, AIDS (as thought to be caused by, or at least linked to, the HIV viruses) does not kill. It is a weakened, insulted or deficient immune system that allows normally trivial

Key principle

diseases to kill. The key principle is 'weakened immune system'. The treatment opportunity alerted by isolating that key principle is: strengthen the immune system of sufferers. At time of writing, the most promising treatment possibility is 'strengthening theory', that is, growing, in culture, strong 'T cells' taken from people not succumbing to known HIV infection and administering them to known sufferers.

To use this opportunity treatment method: Identify the main point behind an idea. If it's no use in one context, it may be useful in another. In which context could the main point be useful? If you can't get agreement on what the main point is, you need to simplify the concept. If you still can't agree, work on whatever key points come up. Maybe the key point is changing depending on in which context the idea is being applied. Take the key point and look for beneficial ways of applying it, or contexts in which it could become beneficial.

Exercise: Identify the key principle behind each major industry group.

Focus on area of strength

What is the strongest part of the idea? How can you enhance it further?

Build on it

In the same way that the abacus was succeeded by the slide rule, build on and enhance the idea by seeking a logical successor.

Action phrase it

Apply action phrases to the idea. And ask how the idea is improved by the action.

The AID method: Advantages/Interesting/Disadvantages

This method is designed to counter instant judgement and create a wider view of opportunity ideas. If you run each idea past the AID method, you'll be forced to go beyond your gut reactions and prejudices. The principle is that you should identify the advantages, interesting aspects and disadvantages of the idea being treated.

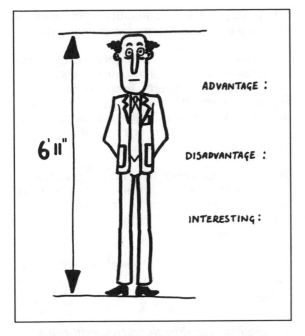

Very tall people – say 6'11" and above – have Advantages: status, impact (sales advantage) . . . ; Disadvantages: door heights 6'6"!, clothes purchase . . .; Interesting Aspects: different view from the rest of us.

What are the advantages, interesting aspects, disadvantages of the idea? What are the advantages in terms of . . .? What is interesting about this idea in terms of . . .? What are the disadvantages in terms of marketing, production, the competition, the customers' perception, long-term strategy, and so on? Collate the views of those involved.

Often treating an idea in this or other ways sparks off better ideas. Seeing other people's interpretation of an idea can enable you to generate improvements. See Build on . . . and Lily pads.

Exercise: Compile a list of factors against which you will conceive the advantages, interesting aspects and disadvantages.

Focus on area of weakness/Tao tactics

Identify the weaknesses in the idea. How can you ameliorate them so they are tolerable? (Like selling your old tyres to . . .) What are the natural forces that the idea could be modified to flow with?

Disadvantage into advantage

Identify the serious problems with the idea.

How can you turn that disadvantage into an advantage? (Remember the salmon.)

Lily pads for a frog

There are two ways to use this treatment method.

Lily pads I

Examine what other possibilities the idea being treated gives you access to. In the same way as the 'build on it' strategy uses ideas as stepping stones to generate other ideas, this method requires you to enhance your idea by examining where it could lead (not what the benefits are). To carry on the metaphor – which pads can you now hop to that were out of reach or out of sight before you had this idea. Someone may see an opportunity to do up the empty

Lily pad jumps

property next door. If the project is profitable s/he may then have unwittingly started a career as a property developer. The next opportunities for our new property developer (with the usual under-funding problems) are probably limited to flat conversions, refurbishments and perhaps small single building plots.

As the business grows, larger deals become accessible, but the smaller deals that were necessary to start up become progressively less economically viable. In other words, the lily pads that can be jumped on to at any time change, depending on which pad you are currently on. Which leads to the second use of this method.

Lily pads II

Take your idea and place it on various pads and look around as above. Which circumstances would the idea work in? What pad provides the optimum opportunities from that idea? What could the idea lead on to from that position? What other opportunities flow from it? What benefits are only available in hindsight (that is, after you have made the jump) that weren't available before.

Exercise: Draw on a large sheet of paper a series of circles representing lily pads to use with this method.

Moving epicentres

Surround the core of the idea with its associated elements; use each of these to form a new epicentre, and in turn surround each of these with associated elements. Take each epicentre in turn and ask: how can we improve this component of the idea?

The UFP method: Uniqueness/Functionality/Pluses

A variation on the AID method with exactly the same objectives in mind. You are seeking to identify the unique aspects, the functionality angles and the pluses of the idea. The repetition of pluses and advantages in the two methods concerned is intentional; having looked at

'uniqueness and functionality', you may be able to see previously unseen advantages.

As an example of the UFP method in action, let's take the concept of a solar cell. Its uniqueness is that it's an energy source with no moving or wet parts. Its functionality is its usability anywhere in the world. Its pluses lie in it being a free energy source after the initial payment and in it being maintenance free.

What is unique about this idea/suggestion? In how many ways could it be functional? What are the advantages? In what ways could we make it more unique, more functional, more advantageous?

Exercise: Devise a UFP sheet (which can be copied) to aid your use of this treatment method.

Wishful thinking/creative ignorance

Who is completely ignorant in the field of the idea that you could ask for suggestions for improvements? What would be your best fantasy for the idea?

Spell it out

Have the originator of the idea state exactly

Spell it out

The UFP method

what s/he means. Have them be extremely simplistic about every aspect of the idea. If others wish to assist in the explanation, so much the better.

Often ideas, when formed, are incomplete or only partially clear in the mind of the originator. Frequently, brilliant ideas can be sensed but remain trapped behind thinking muddled by the excitement of knowing that something wonderful is coming to the surface of the mind. Being asked to spell out the idea to one's peers encourages clarity and may also facilitate further development of thinking as the notion is presented.

DO NOT judge or pass negative comment on the idea as it is unfolding and, perhaps more importantly – make it clear to the person spelling out the idea that you will not do so (this will help minimize any possibly inhibiting tension, thereby maximizingcreativity).

Build ideas in/symbiosis/partnership

How can you enhance the idea by building it into or combining it with some other idea/service/product? For instance, can you combine it with some idea brought in from abroad? With what will the idea form a mutually beneficial relationship? Who or what would make an obvious partner?

Network knitting/piggybacking/tap in to others' resources

In what way can you make the idea more powerful by somehow linking it into some network or other? Can you piggyback the idea on something? How can you enhance the idea by tapping into others' resources?

Information available/information required

Treat an idea as a resource which requires an input of information. Doing so will encourage a constructive approach to further development despite any lack of information. The input of what further information would develop the idea? What do you need to know to carry out the idea? What do you need but do not know? Is the information you require available? If the information is not available, what kind of educated guess would suffice until such time as the idea can be intellectually

developed to the next stage?

Objective setting

What would be the objective you would set for the idea? Look at the objective: how can you alter the idea to make it more likely to achieve its objective?

Working backwards/the something method

Working backwards from the end-point the idea aspires to, what improvements can you see along the road? I want something to improve the idea; what could it be?

Convince/satisfy me, share the background assumptions with me

The same clarification objectives apply in this strategy as applied in the 'spell it out' strategy. As the title suggests, what you do here is to say to the originator of the idea, 'Convince me' or 'Satisfy me' or 'Share the background assump-

tions with me'. You are trying to force further and probably clearer thinking on the part of the idea generator. The process may also give you some ideas to contribute to the opportunity.

Define for me

Here the idea is treated by the originator outlining the objectives, advantages, problem gaps, and uncertainties. What are the objec-

Define for me

tives? advantages? problem gaps? uncertainties? Show me which direction you are trying to go in.

In a similar way to 'Convince me', you are trying here to get the person with the idea to lay down the opportunity in as clear a way as possible. The slightly different emphasis on definition may give an alternative route to clarity, or even further development.

Reminder and summary

The main benefit of enhancing ideas is that you take them closer to being profit-bearing – *before deciding* which is likely to be the most prof-

itable. In addition, you may also come up with an opportunity better than the original idea.

Remember that at this stage you are not trying to evaluate or judge; in fact, you are seeking to avoid that. You don't need to judge at this point because you know that any idea that fails to measure up can be ruthlessly discarded during the evaluations phase. What you are trying to achieve is the facilitation of the further development of ideas.

Finally, remember that what you have in mind when you enhance your ideas will determine your mental output and therefore what results you obtain. In other words control your inner dialogue, and, ask empowering questions.

Exercise: Devise additional, perhaps better, ways of treating ideas. How can you come up with treatments of your own?

Exercise: Re-organize the treatment methods in a way that suits you. You may want to batch similar ones together, or conversely keep similar ones apart so you get two bites at the same cherry.

Exercise: Devise additional empowering questions for each enhancement method.

Exercise: Rewrite the explanation of each method (or any methods you choose) in a better way than the author has. The process will increase your understanding, your memory, and your chances of generating new and better enhancement methods.

Exercise: Do the above exercise for any part of the book you feel is especially important.

Exercise: Take the ideas you generated from the seeking, spotting section and treat or enhance them with the methods shown.

PART II

Evaluating and implementing opportunities

5

Techniques of evaluation

Introduction

Having generated and enhanced a collection of ideas, you now need to evaluate them in order to separate those usable by you from those which are not.

The process of identifying high-potential opportunities highlights one of the biggest differences between normal business problem-solving thinking and Opportunity thinking: to obtain results when dealing with problems you must look for solutions. To achieve through opportunities, you must look for benefits.

- Solutions are judged on the basis of 'will it work and how much will it cost?'
- Opportunities are judged on the basis of the benefits they can bring if they can be made to work.

An opportunity will only be pursued and turn out successful if all parties involved in it are convinced of the benefits to be gained. WHEN EVALUATING OPPORTUNITIES THE BIGGEST SINGLE CONSIDERATION IS THE POTENTIAL BENEFITS.

Evaluating and selecting Ops

Conventional risk assessment and other financial management tools will not work as a means of assessing seriously innovative opportunities. However the closer an opportunity comes to being a standard management decision, the more likely these tools are to work.

There is another factor which is extremely important: the level of commitment in those implementing the opportunity. It is critical to the outcome.

There is, therefore, a need to have strategies for evaluating the potential opportunity AND the commitment level of those likely to develop it.

Who evaluates

There are several possible structures with which to evaluate ideas (or indeed to make any other decision), all of which you are probably familiar with: unilateral decision making by one person, collaborative decision making by a group, bargaining decision making by two people or 'teams'. The best decision-making structure will vary between companies and between the various kinds of ideas and their proposed implementation method. As a rule – the choice of decision-making style should be made on the basis of which method will obtain the highest level of commitment in those most likely to influence the outcome of the decision. (See the Commitment section at the end of this chapter for a more detailed explanation.)

Evaluation methods

- Spell out the benefits – ALL of them
- Create a benefits check list
- Approval and rejection
- Investment size
- Cost likelihood – benefit possibilities
- Leadership rating
- USPs and UMPs
- Gut reactions
- Qualitative factors
- Customer experience profiling
- Time profile
- If strategy
- Cut offs
- Dry runs, pilots, cut-offs
- Map out the scenarios
- Matching
- Market fit

- Commitment
- Comparison of survivors
- Barriers analysis

Consider your idea against each of the methods. Some ideas can be judged by all the methods; other evaluations may simply be inappropriate. Pick and choose from the evaluation methods to suit the idea, your personality and company environment.

In using the methods, have absolute confidence in your decision making. Being confident and committed to achieving results is more predictive of success than the methods used to get there.

Spell out the benefits – ALL of them

What are the overt and covert benefits? Both for the company and the individuals involved? Individuals often have stronger reasons to support an idea than the generator of that idea. Similarly with departments. Only when ALL the benefits are spelled out can true evaluation take place.

Spell out the negative benefits

As distinct from cost, the negative benefits are the non-financial prices to be paid in pursuing an opportunity. What will be the negative benefits to the company? To each department? To each individual?

Identifying the negative benefits to an individual or department will uncover any motives they have for rejecting the idea.

Spell out the benefits

Spell out the latent and manifest benefits

The manifest benefits are easy to see, and they are likely to have a foreseeable 'pay date'. But the latent benefits are less visible. For instance, an opportunity that you have given the go-ahead on may not produce a return, the opportunity may not develop as hoped, the manifest benefits may not manifest themselves. But the latent benefits may be even more valuable.

You will have acquired some information about the opportunity area concerned; you will have signalled to your staff that initiative is encouraged; you will have developed your staff's skill and confidence to take innovation risks.

There are other latent benefits when the opportunity goes to plan. To make a reasoned judgement you need to know as many of the benefits as possible. Spell out the latent and manifest benefits for both a positive and a negative outcome.

Focal point

Following an opportunity policy will provide a focal point at a personal, departmental and corporate strategic level. It will bring all the benefits that objective setting brings and many more besides.

Create a benefits check list

It might look like this:

Create a benefits checklist

- What are the benefits?
- How do they arise?
- How large are they?
- On what do they depend
- In what ways could they fall short of expectations?
- On what assumptions are the benefit projections based?
- When . . .?
- Who . . .?

Devise the questions to suit the idea, the market, the company, the . . . and the checklist must include:

- Latent and manifest benefits;
- Focal point benefits.

Approval and rejection

This strategy is both a means of judging your ideas and your evaluations.

Approval and rejection

All reasons for either approval or rejection of all ideas must be spelled out clearly and documented. Doing so provides several benefits:

1 Everyone involved will know the reasons for whatever decision is reached, which in turn provides two benefits:
   a) If the idea is rejected, those detrimentally affected by the decision will know that their idea has been given fair and reasoned consideration, and are likely to respect the decision and the decision makers.
   b) If the idea is accepted, everyone involved will have the same understanding which will make team work,

85

cooperation and strategic focus easier.
2 You will have a means of assessing your company's Op-Spot performance (more on this later).
3 It will also give you clues to the unconscious or covert evaluation requirements of your Op-Spot programme. Having brought the covert into the open, you can then examine and, if appropriate, challenge and modify previously unstated but commonly held assumptions (epistemes).

Investment size

How large is the necessary investment in the idea? How does that fit in to the company's available resources? If it does fit, is it justifiable to have that amount of funding tied up in a speculative venture? Would it be wiser to have smaller amounts invested in several ideas? If you can't use a large- scale opportunity idea, could you sell it on? Or should you set up a new independent division of the company and seek venture capital to develop the idea, thereby minimizing the risk to the company?

Cost likelihood v. benefit possibilities

If you are going to use conventional analysis, ask yourself can the estimated costs be predicted with sufficient accuracy to make a sensible cost benefit analysis? If not (and that is likely since the nature of opportunities is that you can never tell what it will take to turn them into reality), you should use another assessment method. If you can predict, then quadruple whatever figure you arrived at. Hardly any project in history of any value has ever come in under the original costing. The UK–France channel tunnel looks like coming in on a multiple of 5 (before reaching 'breakeven').

Leadership rating

An idea that would give you absolute leadership in your industry is unlikely to be rejected if making it a reality is humanly possible. An idea that gives you leadership to a lesser but still significant degree would probably still be pursued. The less the degree of leadership offered by an idea, the lower its likelihood of acceptance. Assess the leadership quotient of the big ideas. The smaller scale ideas (such as minor quality or efficiency improvements) ought not to be judged by this method.

Exercise: Compile a means of judging the level of leadership a new product or service would have.

USPs and UMPs

The Unique Selling Proposition (USP) is the unique reason a customer would buy your product or service in preference to all the other options on the market. What is the USP of the idea being proposed? Is it really unique?

The Unique Marketing Principle is a distinctive marketing image that customers want to be associated with that will help sell the product/service. What is the UMP for the idea being considered? Is it unique enough, positive enough? If you can't find a positive answer to these questions, will your customers?

You may not have a UMP at this stage of an idea's development. If so, ask the idea generator to gain whatever assistance s/he needs to formulate a UMP before re-submitting the idea for evaluation.

Gut reactions and revealed preferences

Most of us, in our early years, choose careers on the basis of a preference that had been revealed by some event or influence. Our minds have a certain way of telling us what we want and prefer. Many successful entrepreneurs have made incredibly successful decisions on the basis of a gut reaction. There is nothing wrong with making these decisions from primitive instincts reaction; we've all done it. It often seems to be a good strategy –

as long as you are honest with yourself and admit that the decision was made on a primitive level.

Paradoxically, gut reactions may in fact be very high level processes: previously learned, possibly non-vocalized experiences, may be 'speaking' to us from the most sophisticated parts of our minds.

Qualitative factors

The reasons for accepting an idea may have nothing at all to do with whether or not it works. You may assess that the qualitative benefits for pursuing an idea justify any quantitative costs involved, for example morale, training, unity of purpose . . . (See also spelling out the benefits – latent and manifest.) What will the qualitative benefits be? How valuable are they? Do they alone justify pursuing the idea?

Customer experience profiling

A customer's naive purchasing needs are often quite different from the sophisticated needs of the same user some months or years later. From your sales records and a little existing customer market research, you can compile a profile on the changing experience levels of your customers.

Compare the product/service idea against your knowledge of your customers' average

experience profile. Compare it against the sizes of each of the market segments (if appropriate) that reflect the differing levels of customer sophistication. Does the idea allow sophisticated users to move up a stage or two? Does the idea allow the user with simple needs to avoid paying for functions/facilities/services s/he does not need or want?

Time profile

What is the likely time profile for developing the Op? Can it be implemented quickly or is it a long-term Op? Are you looking for short- or

Time profile

long-term Ops? If you have a good idea, but not on the time-scale you are after, could you pass it on to someone else in the company who could use it? What about the options mentioned above? Could you sell it to another company? Or set up a separate company to develop the idea?

If strategy

The 'if' evaluation strategy works by highlighting all the crucial decision points and assessing their feasibility of success.

Most successful innovations have to go through a series of 'ifs' to reach their destination. In other words, a whole chain of things must take place. Construct an 'If chain' for your idea. It might go like this: the idea will

If strategy

Cut-offs

come to fruition *if* we get the staff; *if* we can find the funding; *if* we can develop the commitment; *if* we can overcome 'that' technical problem; *if* . . . By identifying the 'ifs' you can judge the 'whethers'.

You can use this strategy alongside Barriers analysis, a method at the end of this chapter. Can you see any possible event in the chain which would totally kill the idea? Is there one huge obstacle which, if overcome, would result in near certain success? If so, your thinking could be pointed in the direction of overcoming the obstacle.

Dry runs, pilots, cut-offs

Could the best way of assessing an idea be simply to give it a dry run, or set up a pilot project? Might the best way of selecting between ideas be to set all the contenders on dry runs, even if the dry run is only by intellectual experiment? The best method of evaluation can often be self-evaluation: if it works, it will survive; if it does not, the decision was impartial and automatic. The free market assesses business on that basis.

You could evaluate a potential opportunity by asking those who believe in it to have a go. First, obtain agreement about what would constitute the idea working and not working. Use that agreement to set a cut-off point. The point

may be financial (preferably not, see later), time-, or other target-related.

Map out the scenarios

What are the most favourable, worst, and midway outcomes? There are likely to be more than one outcome in each of the stated categories.

Map out scenarios

If the worst-case scenarios are tolerable and the best-case scenarios are likely to lead to substantial benefits, the opportunity must be a contender for positive evaluation and funding.

When this or any strategy can't give you a clear-cut decision, use one of the others.

Matching

One of the ingredients that will determine your success with a particular opportunity is the fit factor. For instance, it is unlikely that your company has the necessary cash position (flow or reserves) to mine minerals on the moon. The opportunity simply does not fit. Compare opportunities against the various fit factors that will determine their success.

Matching

Does the Op fit:

- the manager's skill, knowledge, attitude, and so on? (#1)
- the cash flow position?
- your market strengths? (#2)
- the production and research facilities?
- the company culture?
- the long-term strategy?

Exercise: State explicitly what your company's position is with respect to the above list. What cash-flow situation you have, what market strengths, and so on.

Exercise: Are the status of the points on the above list going to absolutely determine your Op requirements? Which of them could be altered for a brilliant opportunity idea? For instance, if cash flow was a problem for a particularly good idea, would you move heaven and earth to remove that obstacle? Which of your fit factors are rigid and which are flexible?

Personal matching (#1)

Elaborating on 'Does the Op fit the manager?', it is worth noting that sometimes the opportunity generated is due directly to the factors that produce a personal match. As in the case of Andrew Hallidie, the inventor of the cable car. He invented the device that grips wire rope. His father had invented wire rope some years earlier and Andrew was running their wire rope manufacturing company. Inventing the grip was caused by and clearly matched his personal skills, background and so on.

Similarly Richard Duke, the founder of ChemLawn, was running a garden centre with his father.

For those who are assuming that a family business is a requisite for a good personal match with an opportunity, Robert Maxwell's example should contradict that.

At the end of World War 2, Captain Maxwell was an orphan with no family. His personal interests were languages and science. Combine that with his circumstances and his ambition and it is clear how and why he was able to make the best of the opportunities that came his way. He was working in the Press Department of the Foreign Office helping to run the newly launched German newspapers. From his disposition to make new friends and contacts came an offer of a job as an export agent from Germany's top scientific publisher. Skipping many details, that was the basis for Pergamon Press with its 600+ scientific titles in many languages. A clear personal match.

Details of the kinds of questions to ask to evaluate a match follow in the next few sections, particularly in the section on Commitment.

Market strengths (#2)

Elaborating on 'Does the Op fit your market strengths?', it is obvious that different companies have different opportunities available to them depending on their market strengths.

Some large companies have the opportunities created by economies of scale, others like Saatchi & Saatchi (fourth largest advertising agency in the world at the time of writing) have opportunities available related to the power of scale: the power to do it better, power to be more effective (not just efficient), the power to attract the best talent, to command the lowest priced media space . . .

New business ventures have the power of self-creation, the ability to set up new systems to suit their needs today. They have the power associated with being unfettered by history, the power of the green field.

Sole entrepreneurs have the power of freedom, which gives them advantages above and beyond that of the green field. It gives them the power of total flexibility, the flexibility for self-creation.

What powers does your company have? Does the opportunity you are considering match this power? If not, does the potential in the opportunity justify some serious organizational change?

Market fit

As an extension of 'matching', an opportunity should be evaluated against the question: does it fit the market? Is there a real need? How can you verify it? Does the customer's perceived value justify the price you need to charge to have acceptable margins? Will the required marketing cost per sale leave the price at a level the customer is willing to pay?

Will your company have credibility in that product/service? Will you have leadership in the benefit given?

Some executives are extremely dismissive of market research and marketing research. And they can cite some stunning examples of how first-rate companies lost many millions after following some research conclusion or other (the Ford Edsel, for example). The empowering approach to take is to be positively uncertain about market fit, to acknowledge the need to do research but be sceptical of the results that are produced.

Many, very large and extremely well-managed companies have failed to consider market fit before investing telephone numbers of money in new products. In the UK alone there are

Market fit?

150–200 accidental deaths per year from paracetamol, with another 20 000 non-fatal accidental overdoses. The problem is that paracetamol is known to cause serious liver damage at O/D quantities.

One manufacturer (name withheld) spotted a market for a variety of paracetamol that contained its own antidote to overdose. If the drug could work, it would save many lives and cut the cost of treating the 20 000 cases a year. Clearly a need and substantial benefit existed.

When the drug (Pameton) eventually came to market it totally failed. Why? Because of the price. It sold, or rather didn't sell, at six times the price of paracetamol. What had gone wrong? The company hadn't established whether the market was prepared to pay the price necessary to make a profit and cover the development costs. The market was not willing. Does your new idea's potential market want to pay the price you need to go ahead?

Exercise: What other criteria can you devise that will help you assess market fit?

Commitment

The level of commitment to making an idea work is highly predictive of its likelihood of success. Along with commitment, the quality of the idea and the quality of people, a predictive three-dimensional cuboid grid can be formed. Three-dimensional graphs are awk-

People Quality

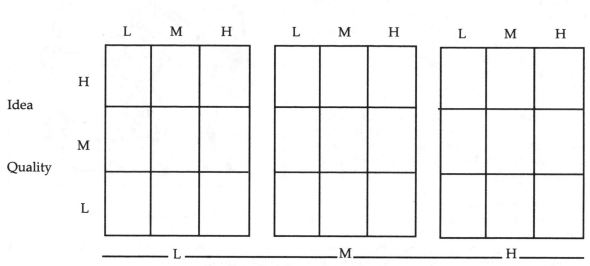

Idea

Quality

Level of Commitment

ward to interpret. Expressed in two dimensions, you can see how important commitment is. Or at least you will do after you've completed the next exercise.

Exercise: Estimate the percentage success rates in each of the boxes formed at the top of this page. H, M and L stand for High, Medium and Low.

A high-quality idea, implemented by high-quality people with a high level of commitment is extremely likely to succeed. Often a poor-quality idea brought to market by fairly average people with high-level commitment will be highly successful.

Commitment is the strongest predictor of success. With commitment, you can overcome weakness in the other two dimensions. But without commitment, the highest levels of the other two dimensions will be ineffectual against the first major barrier.

A person's commitment level is a statement of three parts of their thinking: it reflects their perception of the reality of a situation, indicates their perception of how much control they have over their environment, and how positive or negative their mind set is. A person's commitment level, basically, reflects their faith in the future of the idea; it demonstrates what they foresee or prophesy.

We know that prophecies do more to create the future than predict it. Having a committed

optimist on your team has predictable results. Conversely having a 'doomsayer' on your opportunity team is likely to lead to his/her gloomy predictions coming true.

Handling non-commitment and misuse of evaluation methods

Any of the above evaluation methods could be used negatively by someone who wants to justify not going ahead with an opportunity for whatever reason(s).

A strong, negative case presented well by an articulate, well-informed manager can kill an opportunity at any stage. Should that be a reason to let the opportunity idea die or should it be a reason to let someone other than the negative manager develop it to a stage where it is clearly go or no-go? Op-Spotting should be a positive process throughout and as long as an idea has a champion it should be given a chance or at the very least, not thwarted.

Those known to be negative towards an idea should be dropped from its further development – they would otherwise demoralize those who have the commitment and determination to make it work. There should be no public disgrace from being dropped from an idea team. The individuals concerned should be encouraged to find an idea they do believe in. Indeed they should be helped to understand that it's in their best interests that they be dropped because they would almost certainly fail later if they do not have their heart in the idea.

How to identify high-level commitment to an idea

- Did s/he come up with the idea (directly or indirectly)?
- Has s/he contributed significantly to its development?
- Has s/he got a personal interest in the product/service?
- Does the idea tie in with his/her plans for the future?
- Has s/he experience with the kind of business it would form?
- Does their skill profile match the success factors of the New Business Venture (NBV)?
- Are the tasks ones which they would enjoy?
- Are the people the NBV will attract, those s/he enjoys working with?
- Does s/he like and understand the potential customers?
- Is there any evidence of 'being captivated by the idea' for example spare-time work on it?

Comparison of survivors

Of all the ideas that have reached this stage, which and how many are to be adopted? Compare them for: probability of achieving their objectives, the size of possible returns, the longevity of return, and the risk of an investment resulting in no return, or worse skill, a total loss of investment.

Remember that when evaluating opportuni-

Comparison of survivors

ties, the potential benefits should be the largest consideration.

Exercise: Devise a list of criteria against which to compare each idea.

Barriers analysis

Resisters

Conduct an analysis of the possible barriers and forces resisting your ideas. Where are the barriers likely to be? Who? Where? What? When are the barriers likely to occur? Which could you overcome? Which could others overcome?

Assisters

Conduct an analysis of the possible assistance you could obtain. Ask the who, what, where, when, how, why, of all assistance possibilities.

Objectives assessment

Having looked at the possible help and hindrance, are the objectives realistic? Can the barriers be overcome? But before you decide NO, ask one final question:

Is it achievable by a determined entrepreneur?

If there is no possible human way they can be overcome, your evaluation decision is obvious BUT – and here is the acid test – if a lone entrepreneur like Henry Ford/Walt Disney/ Aristotle Onassis (etc., etc., etc.) decided to make this idea work, could they do it? Bear in mind that for every one of this kind of person, there are perhaps 100 000 000 others, many of

Difficulties

whom will be saying: 'Can't work!' 'Impossible!' 'You'll never raise the finance!' *ad nauseam.* Could you find someone in your company with this level of motivation? Or could you locate someone whose motivation could be enhanced to this level by an appropriate remuneration system?

Exercise: Take your ideas from the previous section on Treating ideas and evaluate them using the above methods. Try to come through with two ideas, so you have sufficient material for the next sections.

Exercise: Try to come up with some better and additional means of evaluation.

Evaluation summary

The two most important points in this section are:

1 When evaluating opportunities look for the benefits that can be obtained. Whatever evaluation method you are using, always ask 'What benefits can this opportunity bring us?'
2 The level of commitment is crucial to, and predictive of, the likely success of an idea.

Exercise: Which of the enhancement methods could be used directly or with a little alteration as evaluation techniques?

Exercise: Apply the same question to the External, Internal and Psychological strategies for generating ideas.

Now that you can choose ideas, you'll discover when you try to do something with them, you will find this happening frequently. (See Figure 138.)

The next section will give you a brick by brick guide to the barriers you are likely to encounter when trying to take your hard-earned ideas further.

Barriers to Op-Spotting

93

6

Overcoming barriers to implementation

Introduction

As with an Olympic hurdler, it only takes one badly cleared hurdle to kill your chances of opportunity success. But unlike the hurdler, your barriers are not always regularly distanced; they aren't equally easy to clear; they aren't always visible; you can't always tell whether or not you've cleared them; and anyone involved can add or change barriers as you go along. Barriers can also take any size, shape or form you care to imagine, and talking of imagination – the barriers might not even be real!

With so many obstacles in the way of every opportunity, why does anyone bother to set up a new company or develop other products/services for an existing one?

Why?

The potential rewards are ENORMOUS!

What are the barriers and how can you overcome them?

The barriers fall into three categories:

- Personal
- Organizational
- Environmental

The next section on Implementing and developing opportunities contains a series of guidelines and pointers to creating an optimally opportunity-sensitive organization. Many of these points are directly designed to overcome the barriers described. However, most organizations have their own unique philosophy and characteristics to the extent that only a knowledgeable 'insider' can decide on the best way to eliminate barriers. This section therefore seeks to help you become aware of what barriers exist. How to overcome the barriers is largely up to you, but methods to overcome the universal and very common barriers will be offered. The more complicated and culturally dependent barriers must be left up to you.

Barriers

95

Personal barriers to Op-Spotting

There are five categories of personal barriers:

● Fears
● Reasoning problems
● Op-Spot conflicts
● Identity/role problems
● Self-fulfilling prophecies

Fears

Fear seems to be the most dis-empowering of all barriers because it is an internal and largely subjective experience. Fear is also the most easily created barrier. Fortunately, management can create the circumstances in which fear is minimized. Knowing what those fears are will help you decide how to alleviate them.

People have fears:

● of failing
● of appearing stupid
● of being laughed at
● of being thought odd
● of not conforming (herd mentality)
● of being fired/losing one's pension etc.

Fear barriers

Dealing with fear barriers

Fear of failing: Successful people direct their fear of failure into providing more motivation to be successful. But, paradoxically, successful people have more failures than failures do. Why? Failures don't try and therefore don't succeed. Whereas successful people see failure as a necessary and regularly used tool in their achievement tool-box.

Few, if any members of staff will admit to being paralysed by fear of their supervisor's reaction, but many are, especially when they are in risky or unfamiliar commercial territory. The role of management, in this situation, is to make it clear that opportunities 'not going to plan' are to be expected.

It may also help to point out the 'failure record' of some of history's all-time achievers. Edison failed to find the right way of creating the electric light bulb a thousand times! Abraham Lincoln lost 18 elections before becoming President of the USA. How many contemporary politicians have stayed around who have lost a third of that number?

Fear of appearing stupid: The Wright Brothers were accused of being stupid, ignorant dreamers. How many other high achievers have been treated with the same derision, only to see their critics arriving at the scene of the success, like flies round XXXX . . . to claim some of the credit? Who ends up looking stupid then?

Fear of being laughed at: What intelligent and knowledgeable person who knows the risks inherent in innovation is going to laugh at someone who has the vision and confidence to try? Only the jealous, commercially naive, or emotionally spineless would laugh. Is laughter from those sources worth worrying about?

Fear of being thought odd: The inventor of the now world-famous Lotus Bike, Mike Burroughs, a self-taught engineer, was thought odd. It didn't stop him revolutionizing the performance bike industry. What kind of person would think a person who is trying to improve his company, country or even humanity is odd? A very strange person indeed.

Fear of not conforming: Or rather, fear of being excluded from one's peer group. This is probably the toughest fear barrier for the normal individual to overcome. Many of us have seen (or experienced firsthand) the pressure from mediocre peers who plead with a high achiever to 'Slow down, you're making the rest of us look bad'. Only by creating a culture where excellence is expected, where excellence is the norm, where achieving it and supporting those who achieve it is rewarded, can management remove the fear of exclusion in the high performer.

Summary of fears

While many anxieties are purely imaginary, some may be well-founded and quite reasonable. For instance, if you really are in danger of being fired for being entrepreneurial to the benefit of your company – you owe it to yourself, your family, and your country to leave and find a company that will respond well to your initiative level. If you are a senior executive, be aware that if you block a good idea (or even one that seems to you to be nonsense), you could find the person you block heading up a new division in one of your competitors' companies. It might also be worth noting that economic history is littered with dead companies whose cause of death was to refuse to accept an enthusiastic employee's idea. The employee seems invariably to go on to be a mega-entrepreneur and sets up a new, even more successful company than his/her last one. More on this later.

Exercise: Which fear barrier(s) could apply to you? What do you propose to do about it or them?

Exercise: Analyse your company culture and place the above fears in order of priority from the point of view of inhibiting Opportunity Spotting in your company.

Exercise: Now decide how you can remove or lessen the two highest fears on your priority list. You might want to do this exercise after having read the Developing and implementing section.

Reasoning problems

- Analysis superiority prejudice
- Logic trap
- Intelligence trap
- The cult of instant judgement
- Listening to 'experts'
- Stereotypes and prejudices
- It's only a short-term solution
- Thinking style
- Head games I
- Head games II

- Lack of focus
- No method
- Too many methods

Each of us has individual reasoning characteristics in the same way we have physical and personality characteristics. Indeed each of these may influence the other. Several factors influence reasoning behaviour: it can be trained, it can also be habit-formed, and much of it is determined by environment and experience. That does not concern us here. What does concern us are the negative factors (specifically reasoning barriers) which we can positively influence in order to maximize opportunity-sensitive thinking. Following is a list of reasoning barriers that can be positively influenced.

Analysis superiority prejudice

There is a widespread assumption in most organizations that analysis is somehow superior to all other forms of reasoning. Analysis is rewarded. Executives and others are trained from an early age to solve problems analytically. That makes it very hard for them to be spontaneous and creative. Analysis presents barriers in several other ways.

1 It is checkable, verifiable, and therefore more likely to be accepted than creative thinking of any type. Managerial staff have to some extent been trained to distrust creativity.

Analysis is rewarded

2   Its absence is attributed to lack of skill, education, knowledge, ability, managerial potential . . .

3   People who have a good idea, but who are disinclined towards analysis, are culturally discouraged from putting forward their idea.

4   People who are inclined towards analysis who have a good idea in the vague formation stage of thinking are discouraged from putting the idea forward, in full knowledge of the reception that a 'half-baked idea without any supporting evidence' will be dismissed.

Analysis is not superior. It is, however, necessary, but as only one of many mental tools. Instinct, gut feel, inspiration, emotional attachment and others are useful too. But analytical types find the unpredictability and uncontrollability of these methods a real turn-off from using them. The way to integrate and accept these methods is to decide to be positive about the uncertainty they entail. Decide to think 'I'm uncertain how I'll come up with an idea but I'm positive I will'.

Logic trap

This and the next reasoning problem are very similar to the analysis barrier. The power of logic is in its attractiveness. If someone puts forward an idea in a series of logical steps leading to a very rational conclusion, it can be extremely difficult to resist the conclusion. Most of us have witnessed the power of logic and try to capture it for ourselves. But we can

be captured, trapped into trying to solve a problem with logic long after it will have become clear to any outsider that the strategy is simply not going to work. Some other method must be used. You can make a logical decision to abandon logic and use one of the creative strategies available to you.

Intelligence trap

Bees, if trapped in a jar with light at the closed end, will do the intelligent thing: try to escape by heading for the light. Flies have no such intelligence and wander around at random, eventually finding freedom.

It is not intelligent to move away from the light. It is not intelligent for an employee to pursue an idea which puts their job at risk. It is not intelligent to spend time on an opportunity if the boss is going to ask why they have been 'wasting' time and not doing what they

Intelligence trap

are paid for. It is not intelligent to pursue an idea behind the scenes if you have been told by your boss to dump it.

Opportunities are like the bee in the jar. Because an employee will usually take the intelligent path towards the light (their income and job), the opportunity will eventually die. If you don't want an organization full of dead bees, make it intelligent for your employees to chase light-emitting opportunities.

Logic trap

Compliance with rules

Company managers are trained to play by the rules. Climbing the career ladder is dependent, in the early stages at least, on doing as one is told and doing a better than expected job. That background makes spotting opportunities difficult. Being creative requires a certain amount of rule breaking, or at least, bending.

Rules barriers

Most people in most countries break the driving speed limits when it is safe to do so. In the UK, virtually no one complies with the 30mph speed limit in towns and cities. *En masse*, they choose when it is wise and safe to follow the limit, and when it is to be ignored. Similarly with commercial rules, once the principle behind them is understood, a choice can be made as to when and if the rules are followed.

It is wise and safe to break them if you can present a good case for your actions. Seeking to innovate, provide options for product succession, ensuring the survival of your company ought to be good enough reasons to break the rules. If they are not – leave, and work for someone for whom those are good reasons. If most staff and executives refused to work in organizations that stifled and penalized their initiative, they would force a change. Companies would be forced to change their ways, for their own benefit.

Rules can create obstacles to opportunity in

several other ways:

1 Others will put down ideas with reference to the rules, either genuinely or maliciously for various reasons that will be covered later.
2 Ideas will die in the heads of their creator as soon as it is realized that the rules would prevent them going any further.
3 Ambiguity about whether or not an idea would break the rules will create such emotional confusion that the idea will be discouraged before it ever sees the light of day.

The first rule in every policy manual should be: 'Any opportunity or innovation idea that requires any rule in this manual to be broken in order to succeed is automatically acceptable as a candidate for adoption, because if it breaks the rules, it is almost certainly a good idea!'

The cult of instant judgement

Managers are often expected to make instant judgements. Failing to do so is taken to imply that they are not in full possession of all the information they should be. Such expectation makes it easiest to say 'That won't work!' rather than spend any time thinking it through and leaving oneself open to criticism.

Counter this barrier by creating a culture where instant judgement is discouraged when

Instant judgement

it comes to opportunities, innovations and improvements. Let it be known that trying to appear to be clever by making instant judgements is the sign of an opportunity obliterator.

Listening to experts and academics

While at Yale University, Frederick Smith, in a term paper, analysed existing freight services and identified a possible market for high-priority time-sensitive goods. He suggested a typical hub-and-spokes distribution network service. Smith's business professor gave the paper a 'C' and stated that federal regulations would present an insurmountable barrier (sound familiar?) and even if they could be overcome, emerging competition from the major carriers would make success extremely doubtful. Of course we now know that the proposed company, Federal Express, is a huge international success.

How would you like to have such a story associated with your career? Almost as damning as to the A&R man who turned down the Beatles, or the publishers who turned down *The Hitchhikers Guide To The Galaxy* or . . . In fact, in the course of compiling this book, I have come across so many examples of the 'experts' being so completely wrong about so many innovations that another book could have been written. It might be titled 'Innovation: If the "experts" like it, you'd better start worrying'. What lessons do these examples provide?

1 Many (not all) experts are not in tune with markets associated with their speciality, and some have become academics or experts because they can't cut it in the real world. There are contradictions to this rule (for instance Sir John Harvey Jones, the British management consultant, who was head of ICI) but you'll be safest following the rule until you are proven wrong.
2 Listen to academics and experts when they are reporting research findings, on events in the past, explaining phenomena, or teaching well-established methods. Those are the things they are good at.
3 Never listen to them when they are talking about what is and is not possible regarding any innovation; they are not people of action, so you can't expect them to have any credibility when predicting the outcome of your innovative actions. Ignore their discouraging cries on anything remotely related to the future, progress, opportunities, achievement or anything unconventional.

4 Ignore the above three points if you come across an expert or academic who willingly states that s/he can't or won't predict the future; who wants to learn about your vision, about what you can see that they can't; who won't predict whether or not your idea is possible, but who is willing to convey to you all the issues they know of that are likely to be involved or important in determining the outcome of your efforts; or who has spent many years as a practitioner before 'retiring' to academia (like Sir John Harvey Jones).

Stereotypes and prejudices

Stereotypes and prejudices (S&Ps) are desirable. Despite what the 'politically correct' brigade would say, S&Ps are necessary for our mental organization of the world, and it is essential to hold some for your own self-protection. Would you let a child murderer look after your children? Or a multiple bank robber be chief cashier at your bank? Or an infectious disease sufferer give you blood for a blood transfusion?

Some S&Ps are empowering to hold. We need some solid beliefs about people, places and so on to make sensible decisions. But there comes a point where the S&Ps are too broad, too sweeping, too general and they cease to be

Stereotypes and prejudices

empowering and constructive and become actively dis-empowering and self-destructive.

It is difficult for each of us to accept that we have socially undesirable S&Ps, beliefs that have gone too far. And even if we can accept that, we can't always see which are empowering and which are dis-empowering. The dis-empowering S&Ps may create a series of barriers between you and your available opportunities.

We know the S&P barriers exist but what do we do about them? There are several strategies you could use. First, you should ensure everyone on your opportunity team is aware of the negative power of S&Ps, and ask everyone to keep an ear out for S&Ps masquerading as genuine reasons for accepting or rejecting an idea. Second you could analyse your reasons for not pursuing an idea (see the Reasons for approval and rejection evaluation method). Third (if you are able to be ruthlessly honest with yourself), you could take a long look in the mirror and identify all your prejudices and note down a list of those that are dis-empowering. You could consult and add to your new checklist when evaluating ideas. Maintaining an awareness of the likely influence of S&Ps is probably the best and easiest way of overcoming their effect.

It's only a short-term solution

Assume you are a major shareholder in a large company which was in a very competitive market. Assume that industry was highly susceptible to fraud. Some bright spark comes up with a method that is proven to cut the costs of fraud to 1 per cent of the previous level. And the costs of introducing this method would cover themselves many times over (pilot costs excluded) in the first year, at no extra costs to your customers. You would probably assume that you, as a shareholder, would not have to push your employees (the directors of the company) to adopt the new method. Right? Wrong!

The Royal Bank of Scotland (UK) introduced such a system for its customers in 1992/3. Customers' photographs were made part of the credit/charge card. Fraud against those cards whose customers had voluntarily agreed to participate in the pilot scheme was reduced to 1 per cent of the previous level (even the pilot system covered its cost by 150 per cent). Since 75 per cent of fraud occurs at the point of sale, it is not surprising that this system has worked so well. The Bank concerned are

adopting it *en masse*.

At the time of writing, ALL other UK banks, through the bankers' organization, have rejected the idea (publicly on BBC Radio 4) on the grounds that it is 'only a short-term solution'. They are prepared to wait for 'even better technology' to come along at some unspecified date in the future. The preferred option is signature pad pressure recognition. It is not

cheap, not installed in every outlet worldwide, and not even available yet! Rather than implement an acceptable, virtually free solution now, they are going to wait for something even better. 'Even better?' Uh? How much better do you get than 99 per cent, with multiple payback in the first year, and no expensive equipment involved?

Now back to our original assumption – if you were a shareholder in one of these banks, how would you be voting at the next annual general meeting, particularly on the issue of appointment of directors?

Taken to an extreme for the purposes of illustration, the above grounds for rejection would be like the stone-age cave dweller saying, 'Let's not bother with this "wheel" idea for transport. There will be space rockets and jet engines available soon.'

It is inevitable that better methods will evolve in every field. Don't allow 'It's only a short-term solution' to block an opportunity.

Thinking style

We each have our own thinking styles and methods. Our intellectual life is as unique as our personality. In the same way that certain personalities prosper in particular situations, certain thinking styles are more suited to some opportunities than others. And certain thinking styles are more likely to spot some opportunities than others.

By implication, each thinking style has its own inherent barriers to becoming aware of certain kinds of opportunities. If you are aware of your own style and its inevitably large opportunity blind spots, you can take action to restore full vision by changing your thinking, by adding to your thinking repertoire, or by employing someone who thinks in the way you do not. The following categories are for example only, and illustrate the barriers some people face.

Bureaucrat: Bureaucrats make their living by habitually referring to, interpreting and applying rules that some higher authority has laid down. The barrier to be overcome in this kind of thinking is the need to refer to some higher authority or rule book for decision guidance. Accountants have a similar barrier; they are, de facto, historically focused in their thinking: keeping books on what has happened, reporting on how profitable a company has been, reporting on whether a company's historical records are a true and fair representation of what has happened and so on. Recognizing the barrier exists is the first step to overcoming it. Accountants and bureaucrats are excellent at spotting and creating cost savings and system improvements in existing systems, but are not so wonderful at spotting or even supporting future or visionary based opportunities.

Maintenance: Many managers (as opposed to leaders) make their livings by doing what is required to be done to keep things running smoothly. Management tasks are usually centred around maintaining an organization in a stable state. The mental barriers come from the fact that anything that upsets or threatens that stability is frowned on and attacked. (More on this later.) The way to handle this resistance is to flow with it (Tao tactics): managers need to be persuaded that the best way to maintain the department, and the company is to maintain the flow of innovative ideas for product suc-

Thinking styles

cession and ongoing improvement.

Corner shop: Corner-shop thinking is characterized by running a business from a particular location and making the best possible job of obtaining a return from the assets. There is enormous strength in that as a strategy but it blocks the seeking, spotting or creating of ideas that have potential outside the location. The obvious remedy is to consciously decide to think on a wider scale, in a more mobile way.

Entrepreneur: Paradoxically, or even unbelievably, the entrepreneurial thinking style presents barriers to spotting opportunities. Or rather to developing opportunities into anything substantial. Habitual Opportunity Spotters see so many opportunities that they fail to stay focused on one long enough to establish a lasting enterprise. When photocopiers became cost-effective for businesses to purchase, many entrepreneurs set up photocopier dealerships. When faxes came along, they dumped photocopying and moved on. When mobile phones came along, they dumped faxes and . . . The remedy is for the entrepreneur to employ someone to run the established business, while s/he goes off and does what they are best equipped for.

Head games I – Presence of

Knowledge or information can change your mind. Your mind can change, distort, erase . . . knowledge and information. There is a huge number of mental phenomena that can distort our thinking. From selective vision, selective processing, or the more commonly

known selective memory to denial, exaggeration, projection, rationalization, to mention but a few.

Many of the Opportunity-Spotting strategies presented in this book use these phenomena to aid creativity; in that context they are empowering. They become dis-empowering barriers when we unwittingly use them to protect ourselves from emotional pain. We prevent ourselves becoming aware of information which threatens us but which, if used constructively, could contain opportunity-rich facts. If you get hurt, don't put up the barricades; invite the enemy into your camp. As with many of the barriers, simple awareness of its existence can be sufficient to alert you to avoid it.

Head games II – Absence of

Some head games are necessary for emotional survival. In some regards it is necessary to deceive ourselves. Numerous research studies have shown that physically and psychologically healthy individuals play three head games:
1 They have an unrealistic optimism about

the future.
2 They have exaggerated perceptions of personal control.
3 They have an unrealistically positive view of themselves.

Not holding these misconceptions makes you more prone to depression, anxiety and various other causes of under-achievement.

Strange as it may seem, we now have a logical case with which we can argue that it is reasonable to be unreasonable. Eat your heart out, Descartes. It appears that to fail to deceive

yourself in these three ways is to erect a barrier against your future achievement, by physically and psychologically disabling yourself. Any one for head games?

Lack of focus

This is the barrier that is erected when we fail to set ourselves objectives. The much over-quoted phrase, 'if you don't know where you are going you'll probably get there' applies. The simple remedy is to set Opportunity Spotting as an objective. Then set goals for what you want to get from your Opportunity-Spotting activities.

Lack of focus

103

No method or technique for Op-Spotting

This is the barrier we are addressing in this book.

Too many strategies

The exact opposite of the previous one, and a barrier that could be caused by this book. There are so many ways of finding opportunities that it becomes difficult to choose between them. Overcome this information overload by choosing the opportunity strategies that fit your company and personality best. Then use them so regularly that they become intellectual habits. Only you can make that decision.

EXERCISE: Identify one situation from each of the above in which you allowed a reasoning problem to block your progress.

EXERCISE: Which ideas that have been generated in your company recently have been thwarted by someone reasoning in one of the ways listed above?

Op-Spot conflicts

- Familiarity *v* novelty
- Career plan security
- Putting people out of work
- Too much hassle
- Reactive norm
- Acting preferable to thinking
- Not invented here

Once the need for Opportunity Spotting is understood, the consequent motivation in your staff will be extremely powerful. However there are other motivating factors at work in the mind of the average executive, often creating conflicts of interest. Some of the Op-Spotting conflicts follow.

It's easier to stay with the familiar, than to take on the new

Whether we like it or not, most people prefer to work with the familiar than to experience change, the unknown, or other unpredictable ghouls.

Even if you create a 'constant flux culture', some people will continue to resist change. The best way to handle this resistance is to have every job, role, department, function, policy and so on fight for its life on a regular basis. Those that can't explain how they benefit the

Familiarity v. progress

organization NOW (not last year or last month) are abandoned. The only way to be able to justify the existence of any part of the organization is to be constantly changing to meet the current and future needs of the organization and its markets.

Career plan security

Protectionist empire-building is safer for most managers than is risk-taking.

The way most companies are currently structured, there is an active de-motivation from taking innovation risks. And in any event, the time spent pursuing a risky idea could be time otherwise used for building empires.

Remedied as above. If the only route to promotion is to demonstrate good management AND systematic, ongoing improvement, innovation and Opportunity Spotting, then the 'protectionist manager' will have little choice in building his/her empire by doing so.

Putting people out of work

Nobody would forgo an enormous opportunity that could make the lives of millions easier, on the basis that the innovation might put a few people out of work. Would they? Walter Hunt allowed this barrier to make him aban-

Career protection

Reactive v. pro-active

don the sewing machine he had invented a full 16 years before Singer invented his machine. Hunt feared that his invention would make the world's seamstresses redundant. Of course we now know that the seamstresses re-trained in the new methods and ended up several times more productive than they had been before. How do you overcome this barrier? By making three empowering assumptions:

1 Labour markets must be viewed as mobile and flexible.
2 If you don't follow the idea, eventually someone else will.
3 If you don't make the fortune associated with the idea, someone else will.

Op-Spotting is simply too much hassle

On an individual basis it is often difficult for personnel to justify the inconvenience and risks of Op-Spotting to themselves. Of course, too much hassle is a relative term; if the rewards were larger and the risks smaller the perception of staff would be quite different. The job of senior management is to find the point at which 'too much hassle' becomes 'too much lost not to'.

The re-active norm

It's easier for most people to wait for some-thing to react to than it is to be pro-active. How many times have you heard the excuse 'I'm waiting for . . .' when you've asked how something is progressing? What kind of person usu-

ally makes such an excuse? Most of us at some time or other.

The conflict exists in preferring to be reactive, but knowing that being pro-active is likely to obtain better results. We know that pro-active people are higher achievers than reactive types. It is the role of senior management to encourage pro-active employee behaviour to become the norm rather than the exception. Or more dramatically, it is the role of senior management to encourage the view that reactivity is the wave on which mediocrity is borne and pro-activity is the crest on which opportunities are born.

It's easier to act than think

Opportunity Spotting takes a great amount of thought. Most people prefer to act than to think. It's easier and more satisfying to plunge into a task than it is to perhaps spend the majority of the time thinking and planning, for which there is no demonstrable outcome. The financial consequences of such haste runs into millions. Yet most companies encourage it. Employees are frequently pressured by their bosses to 'Show me what you've done' which further increases the motivation to act rather than think. The best remedy to this, as with the other conflicts, is to create a culture which min-

Action v. thought

imizes the conflict and rewards the desired behaviour.

Not invented here syndrome

Sly Gremmlin had great difficulty in accepting that another employee has an idea that is enormously superior to Sly's best. Naturally, he would like to have come up with the idea. Sly finds himself in a career conflict. If the value of the idea is acknowledged, the other party gets all the credit and glory, and probably walks off with 'the prize' as well. But if a means of sabotaging the idea can be found then, well . . . there is still a chance for Sly to come up with a 'biggy'.

Of course Mr Gremmlin is a fictional character. But he needn't be. And it needn't be another employee; it could have been another company. It is not only petty-minded people to whom this pit opens. Intellectual giants have fallen down this hole.

Edison tried to rubbish George Westing-house's AC electricity system on the grounds of safety. In reality, he behaved like that because his DC position was threatened by the obvious superiority of Westinghouse's AC system.

Even today this conflict can kill opportunities for all of humanity. Ten years prior to its acci-dental discovery, Chapman had predicted the existence of carbon-60 (a third form of pure carbon) and he was laughed at. Engineers at Exxon were investigating a dirt problem caused by carbon. Some suggested it was carbon-60, but the idea was dismissed by management. Various scientists around the world were seeking to create this evasive structure in the lab. Several managed to do so, but not in any quantity or for any period of time.

Exxon dismissed the findings as experimental artefacts (not invented here). Eventually Huffman and Krachner discovered how to produce carbon-60. At this point I'd like to report that Exxon then rubbished carbon-60 as worthless, but I can't. The head of research, Kaldor, immediately accepted he had been wrong and set his team to work to find commercial applications for carbon-60.

Having the humility to swallow your pride and live with the fact that someone else was smarter than you could be the most intelligent decision you ever made. And it could pay back handsomely. Good luck, Dr Kaldor and company!

EXERCISE: Be honest here; can you remember a chance you've had to achieve something, but chosen the easy, safe route? When in your past did you rubbish an idea because it was not yours?

Identity/role problems

Frequently people see themselves in a particular role and feel comfortable as long as they operate within the confines of that role. When asked to initiate an Opportunity-Spotting programme, you may see some people erecting this barrier at its most obstructive.

Often people will convince themselves and others that what they are being asked to do as an additional task is already being done, albeit in a different way from that being asked. You may be able to identify 'role rigidity' by listening for the following kinds of statements.

Complacency

'*We* are already doing more than enough of that.'

Complacency is the biggest barrier to the sale of this book. And is a substantial barrier for you introducing an innovative culture. Most executives think they are doing enough. Education is part of the answer, education that 'enough' is not even a start.

Superiority

'Opportunity Spotting is for barrow boys, cowboys and gamblers.'

Many professional managers will tell you that if they had wanted to take risks, they would have become gamblers or worse. As above, the best remedy is education, education that to not take any risks is the riskiest option of all – because the only possible route from there is stagnation and slow decline.

Identity/role problem

Arrogance

'I'm a manager . . . not an . . . e . . . entrepreneur.'

Some employees look down on small-time entrepreneurs, seeing them as criminals who haven't been caught yet. Any activity that is similar to the behaviour of such individuals is frowned on (see above). Again, education is the key. Every company was started by the use of the kind of methods the arrogant frown on. Their jobs were created by someone using the

methods they dismiss.

EXERCISE: Decide what educational measures you can take to counter role rigidity.

Self-fulfilling prophecies

The decisions you make about the achievability of this or that goal tend to make themselves self-fulfilling. Making a negative decision can create an enormous barrier to achievement. The dismissed opportunity is not considered a possibility. You tend to notice things that confirm you were right to dump the idea. Result: non-achievement.

Similarly, if you make a positive decision about an opportunity; it is considered realizable. You notice things that will help you towards achievement. Your mind-set is such that you interpret information as confirming your judgement, you find people, events, items

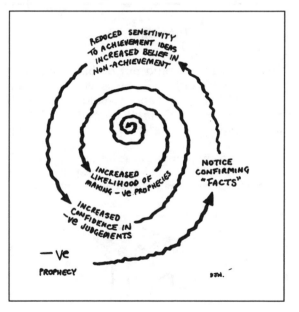

and so on that aid your journey. Result: achievement probable.

EXERCISE: What ideas have you had in the past that you've dismissed and had your rejection confirmed by events only to see someone else actually achieve what you thought was not possible?

EXERCISE: Devise a system whereby each time you reject an Op you analyse yourself to see if your rejection was motivated by any of the above barriers.

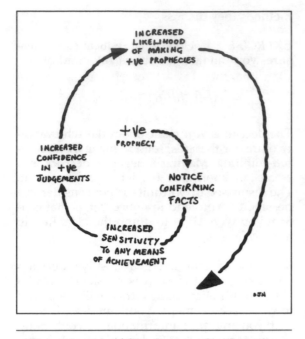

Organizational barriers to Op-Spotting

Introduction

No organization would put up barriers to the process that would ensure its very survival, would it? No organization would shoot itself in the foot, would it? Surely not? OH YES! And deliberately too!

> "... one of the purposes of an organization is to be inhospitable to ... ideas and creativity. The organization exists to restrict and channel ...

behaviour into a predictable and knowledgeable routine. The organization exists ... to create [the] kind of inflexibility ... necessary to get jobs done efficiently". (Theodore Levitt, 1963)

So there are sensible reasons to put up barriers to opportunity spotting: too much change or too rapid a change can kill any organization. It is therefore smart for companies to react against, or at least be cautious of, change.

The opposite is also true: too much stability, or non-change, can kill an organization. The outside world is always in flux and not responding to that change will be fatal.

There must be a sensible balance between these two extremes. Corporate defences (or the corporate immune mechanism) must exist BUT the threshold at which the defences are triggered must be sufficiently high to allow the innovation and Opportunity Spotting necessary for survival to carry on, unimpeded.

Organizational barriers that exist by default, rather than by necessary design, fall into at least three categories:

- Survival today (time pressure barriers)
- Management style (culture-based barriers)
- Op-Spot skills (skill-based barriers)

Survival today

Urgency frequently takes precedence over importance: things which are perceived as urgent are done before, and often in place of, those things which, when not done at all, will have serious consequences. The day-to-day pressures of business survival often make it 'necessary' for tasks that are urgent for survival today to be given priority over those that are important or even essential for survival tomorrow.

For instance, cost cutting and expenditure reduction is seen as urgent. Analogies, like commercial haemorrhaging, are used to dramatize and convey the urgency of applying first aid. The error in that thinking is that it assumes that tomorrow is going to be like today. Cutting costs today is an admirable goal, but not on its own, and not when it is cost cutting on the basis of assumed stability, and certainly not when it is at the expense of survival tomorrow.

The end result of cost cutting can be that limited resources are needed for survival on a day-

Survival today

Management style

Autocratic, 'we know best' style. In these environments conformity is valued more highly than initiative. Executives operating like that should not expect initiative, innovation, system improvements, product succession ideas and the like, because they won't get them. They should expect to waste intellectual resources on an incredible scale. And if by some miracle someone does generate an idea,

Management style barriers

to-day basis and as such are made inaccessible to those interested in longevity needs.

Stakeholder short-termism: Stakeholder needs (such as shareholders looking for a dividend this year) are often short term in nature. Paying that dividend this year may knock on the head the projects that could ensure an enormous jump in the share value of the company next year, not to mention the effect it could have on future dividend growth!

it will always be easiest and safest for the junior managers to say 'No' and kill the idea in its tracks.

If the rewards for putting forward ideas are high and the 'we know best' factor is low, you can expect all of these things and more.

Down-only communication: In which directions do communications run in your company? It might be worth conducting a small-scale communications audit to establish what percentage of communication goes up the ladder and what comes down from the top. The larger the percentage going up in relation to that coming down, the more likely you have a company where the management see it as their role to harness the powers of their staff by supporting them. And the closer you are to

Urgent v. important

having an opportunity-rich culture. If the outcome is 'One way communication – down only', you have a long road to travel. Perhaps the aphorism, 'You have two ears and one mouth; use them in that proportion', doesn't go far enough.

Rigid hierarchical structures: A solid formal hierarchy presents a barrier to opportunities, because every single layer of management presents yet another chance for an idea to be rejected for all the spurious reasons we've covered. Create a separate idea-handling structure of some kind (more on this later).

Information unavailability: How freely available is information in and about your company? If information is openly available, all your staff have access to the information they need to generate opportunities. While you are restricting information for fear of industrial espionage (a sensible precaution), are you also strangling the future you seek to protect? Remove this organizational barrier by finding a way to give your staff the information they need while still controlling how far the information goes.

Bureaucracy (too much): Japanese bureaucrats nearly stifled the early Sony business and their own economic miracle. They refused to allow Masaru Ibuka, Sony's founder, an allocation of foreign exchange to buy a licence for semiconductor technology for transistor radios. The bureaucrats thought the idea silly. Eventually

after phenomenal pressure they capitulated. How would Japan have fared if the bureaucrats had got their way?

To any bureaucrats reading this book (most unlikely!): do you know enough about any field, other than administration, to block a possible future innovation of any size, let alone one that could hold the key to your country's future?

No encouragement for innovation or Op-Spotting: Covered indirectly before, this barrier can be expressed, and have its solution offered by, the single question, 'If management are not interested, why should I stick my neck out?'

Management pressure for results: No experienced management team of international repute would pressurize staff and contractors to complete an innovative project so fast that the success of the project, the lives of many people and the whole future of the organization would be on the line. (Does this line of argument sound familiar? If so, you know what comes next.) Would they? You've guessed it. Yes, they would, Yes, they did. NASA officials put such pressure on the Challenger project team that balanced risk taking was undermined, dissident views were ignored, and seven of the finest young people in the world were lost. A report from a junior engineer that the 'O' ring seals on a rocket booster would not function in low tempera-

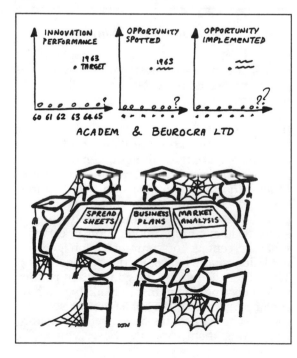

110

tures was ignored and dismissed by higher officials because of the pressure they were under.

Pressure to obtain results can be constructive, but not where it involves suppressing or repressing information crucial to the outcome of a project. By all means put the pressure on. Do so at the same time you take your ear muffs off.

Technology-push prejudice: Prejudices have been covered earlier, but this one warrants special attention. In much of the corporate strategy literature, technology push as an innovative strategy gets a bad press. The process of inventing a new device and taking it to the market is regarded as much too risky to be worth adopting. It is said to be much smarter to wait for the market to demand or pull an invention into conception.

Without entering into a listing of the hundreds of major human achievements that were technology-push inventions, it is obvious that this prejudice is dis-empowering. If someone invents a device, it is because that person wanted to achieve something. There is therefore a *de facto* market of at least one person. And since there are 5 to 6 billion of us, it is unlikely that the inventor had a unique desire. Once invented, the challenge then becomes one of commercializing the idea. Even if the idea is still on the drawing board, it would be preferable to do some basic low-cost market research, to establish whether there is a market for the idea, or even to discover what market

there might be than to dump it on the grounds of technology-push prejudice.

Op-Spot skills deficit

The lack of Op-Spot skills, knowledge, structure is being addressed in this book. It is designed to counter the barrier formed by lack of Op-Spotting skills at an individual and company culture level. Sometimes part of a skills deficit problem can be an abundance of the wrong kind of skill. In general, having too many analytical types kills creative ideas, through the paralysis induced by analysis.

You need to reward creativity as well as the conventionally rewarded analytical thinking. Be wary of having analytical types work on an 'inspiration oriented' opportunity. They will be liable to kill the idea stone-dead if they apply their usual, analytical methods too early in the creative process. Some of the Opportunity-Spotting methods outlined in a previous section DO depend on analysis and those are the methods best used by that kind of person.

Skills arrogance: Strangely, some of the most opportunity-negative cultures are headed by entrepreneurs. They seem to believe that they have a localized monopoly on entrepreneurial thinking. They may indeed be justified in thinking they are the most entrepreneurial in their company (after all they have proven entrepreneurial ability and, *de facto*, anyone working for them has not). But by monopolizing Opportunity-Spotting thinking, many entrepreneurs deny their company access to enormous intellectual resources, at great cost.

Founder's disease: Such people often go on to develop Founder's disease. This is a strange, not rare enough, syndrome. It only afflicts normally dynamic, visionary, change-oriented, opportunity- and results-focused types. The symptoms are strategic myopia and a tendency towards stagnation and protectionism. The prognosis is for the rapid growth of a particularly pernicious substance called 'competitors'. Well-known sufferers of Founder's disease have been Henry 'You can have it in any colour you like, as long as its black' Ford, and Thomas 'AC is unsafe' Edison. More contemporary examples include Frederick Smith, who, when he saw the threat posed to his express envelope service by the rapid spread of the fax, spent $200 million trying (and failing) to develop his own electronic transmission facility.

Protecting your business is smart, but not if it

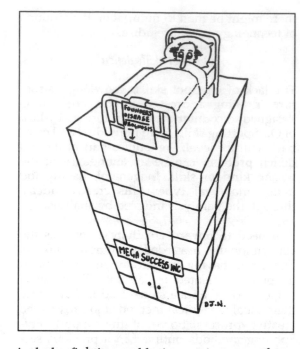

Since many of the environmental obstacles to opportunities are those you deal with on a daily basis, there will be no teaching granny how to suck eggs in terms of how to overcome these barriers. A straightforward memory-prompting list should suffice. For others a more detailed explanation will be offered.

- Bureaucratic constraints
- Changing market conditions
- Disasters
- Entry barriers / costs
- Environmental perfectionists and others
- Human and market inertia
- Known exit costs functioning as entry barriers
- Legal and other regulatory
- Poor venture capital structure
- Prohibitive and excessive costs of raising capital
- Union restrictions
- Tax, price controls
- Tax inequity:
  - You win – you get taxed
  - You lose – tough, not tax-allowable!
- Variable information quality and reliability
- Variable information source reliability

includes fighting and losing against something you ought to be cooperating with and incorporating into your business. Ford eventually had to produce other colours of cars, but only after so many competitors entered his market that he lost what could have been an enormously strong position.

Identifying Founder's disease in oneself is particularly difficult. Like many of the other barriers, being aware of its existence may be sufficient inoculation.

Organizational barriers summary

Even enthusiastic and dedicated staff with high levels of initiative will be thwarted by the above list of management-imposed barriers. Would you continue to work in such a company?

The author's solution to each of these barriers is offered but if you don't like these ideas, make up your own solutions. In doing so, you could do worse than taking the exact opposite position to that contained in the barrier's title and move towards the middle ground between the two extremes. For example, instead of 'down only' communication, move towards two-way communication (as opposed to 'up only').

Human and market inertia

Gas was generally perceived to be reliable (?), safe (?) and relatively cheap by its customers and, naturally, by its suppliers. The gas companies fought tooth and nail to stop Eddison introducing his new electrification scheme. Members of the public were hardly more progressive. If a revolutionary, life-enhancing breakthrough like electric light met with such resistance (excuse the pun), a mere innovation or opportunity will probably have to generate some considerable wattage to succeed. Massive publicity or creeping inclusion are two of the many strategies open to you. (This is where Opportunity Spotting ends and marketing expertise begins.)

Entry barriers/costs

The cost of entering a new business is not just financial. There are several distinct barriers to you being competitive upon entering a new business. You need to overcome them to be as competitive as the established players.

Assuming it isn't a totally new business that no one has ever set up, in which case the barriers to you are pretty much the same as for everyone else.

- Lack of economies of scale: You won't have the economies of scale that your competitors will have.
- Lack of brand identity (Product differentiation): Your competitors will have this; you will have to spend and work hard to acquire it.
- Transition costs: from your current business to the new one.
- Lack of distribution outlets/channels: You may be able to use your existing distribution methods/channels for your opportunity idea. Gillette successfully used its channels to enter the cigarette lighter market.
- Lack of learning curve and historical economies: Your competitors have all sorts of intellectual, system, technology, source, locational and other historical and learning curve advantages. If you can overcome these and still be competitive, you've got a great opportunity idea. In fact, you've probably got a genuine product or process innovation that renders historical advantages useless. (Remember to use the assessment of barriers as an evaluation technique.)

Tax inequity

You win – you get taxed
You lose – tough, not tax-allowable!

In the USA, investing in a 'start up' opportunity, which doubled in value, would after inflation and capital gains tax produce a return of less than 2 per cent, against a possible loss risk of 100 per cent. With odds like that, why bother? Don't! Vote with your money and invest elsewhere. If any government wants to stack the cards against you, there is no choice. People in a free market under those conditions act *en masse* and cause a sudden vacuum in the venture capital market. The effect that has on the economy eventually forces governments to alter their tax policies.

Exit costs

Known exit costs function as entry barriers. Every business has a series of exit costs associated with it. In planning to enter a market, you can minimize this barrier by planning to keep your (possible) exit costs low. For instance, if

you are setting up a new retail outlet, don't buy: rent. If you are entering a volatile and highly labour-dependent market, have short-term, renewable employment contracts rather than permanent employment to avoid redundancy costs (and be ethical enough to tell the staff involved – so that adverse publicity and future recruitment difficulties don't turn out to add an unseen exit cost).

EXERCISE: Which of the above barriers exist in your organization and how do you propose to side-step/remove them?

EXERCISE: Take a look at all the ideas you generated from the previous stages. Which of them were rejected for personal barrier reasons. If the answer is none, examine your navel a little closer!

Barriers summary

EXERCISE: As in the above exercise, which ideas/opportunities were rejected for organizational reasons? What can be done about those blocks?

EXERCISE: As in the above exercise, which ideas/opportunities were rejected for environmental reasons? What can be done about those blocks?

113

Summary

Having listed, outlined and described many of the barriers to successful Opportunity Spotting, we will turn to the next section. As stated previously, only an informed insider can know how best to banish barriers in the way of developing and implementing an opportunity. The next chapter will be a series of checklists and recommendations from each of the major decision-making areas. Some points will have been covered before, and will be covered again to enable you to use the chapter as a stand-alone checklist for creating an opportunity culture.

7

Implementing and developing opportunities

Introduction

Many successful people have uttered a phrase something along the lines of 'Achievement is 1 per cent inspiration and 99 per cent perspiration'. The exact ratio suggested varies from achiever to achiever but the main point is that generating and choosing an idea is the starting point. For that part, you can be given enormous amounts of help and advice. But with the largest and most significant part, only vague guidelines can be offered. The exact 'how to implement ideas' will be and can only be up to you: only you can combine the techniques so far discussed with a knowledge of what will work, or can be made to work in your company.

Coaching opportunities

Decisions to make

Each company should choose its own means of spotting, seeking, creating, enhancing, developing and implementing opportunities, and the cultural context in which those activities will be conducted. But every company will have to make decisions in each of the following areas:

- Opportunity culture creation
- Communication
- Opportunity-gathering methods
- Key roles
- Recruitment, reward and remuneration
- Training and management
- Planning and administration
- Goal setting
- Financial issues
- Measuring innovative performance

One of the biggest decisions in Op-Spotting that you'll never have to make is whether to include bureaucrats in the process.

> PRINCIPLE: Bureaucrats and protectionist managers are the death of innovation, creativity, risk taking and initiative.

Use whatever methods you must to exclude all known bureaucrats from evaluation and implementation stages of Op-Spotting (unless, of course, it is their idea that is being developed). This policy will not be as harsh as it sounds; the individuals concerned will, in the first instance, not opt in to Op-Spotting; their view of it is likely to be dismissive, negative and probably hostile. In the second instance, you already have and are about to obtain other strategies for dealing with bureaucrats and protectionist managers.

An illustrative example of how petty and needlessly destructive bureaucrats can be: The Greek Consul to Rotterdam refused to allow one of Aristotle Onassis' ships to leave the port because a Greek cook had taken ill and under Greek regulations had to be replaced by another Greek cook. Well, you try to find a Greek cook at short notice in Rotterdam, and one who is willing to leave his/her current job and family and sail off at the drop of a hat. Despite the strongest protests, the Consul maintained his refusal.

Onassis invited him on to the ship where he ceremoniously handed the Consul the Greek flag in a brown paper bag, and informed him that the ship was now re-registered under the Panamanian flag and would be leaving port as planned.

The point here is if you can side-step, ignore or otherwise deal with a bureaucrat who is standing between you and an opportunity, you are entirely justified in doing so.

You might well ask: how can you exclude the known bureaucrats and progress killers without alienating them? The answer is that you can't. Indeed you shouldn't try to avoid alienating them. When these people eventually realize that their rule-bound, negative and restrictive attitudes are going to cause them to be left out of the action, they will come round

to your way of thinking. That is certainly the case in a small company. In a larger company, the education process is slower, but that need not matter, because in a larger environment it is easier to avoid such human obstacles all together.

Progress killers can be handled if you can identify them. But how can you identify and nullify the effects of the most dangerous progress killer – the kind who show enthusiasm publicly, but are saboteurs behind the scenes? The American company, 3M, have a great policy for dealing with all attempts to stop an idea. The burden of proof is placed on the person or group who wishes to block an idea. The idea is presumed workable until proven otherwise.

Creating an Op-Spot culture – (general points)

There would be nothing easier than for the author to present a blueprint for the organizational changes needed to create an Opportunity Spotting culture. As already stated, that can only be done by an informed insider using the kinds of ideas contained in this book in conjunction with his/her knowledge of the company concerned. Most of this chapter is aimed at assisting you in achieving cultural change, by giving advice pointers in the specific areas listed above. You can use the principles to draw up your own 'informed insider' blueprint or indeed, to develop and implement a single idea. The more general points behind that advice are that a company should have:

- A tolerance of, and rewards for, risk taking
- A tolerance of diversity in people and thinking
- Freedom to innovate
- Awareness that innovation success must

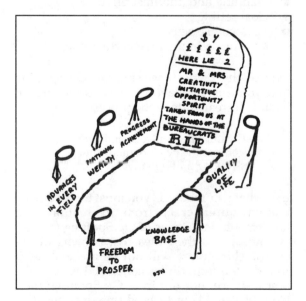

The effects of bureaucracy

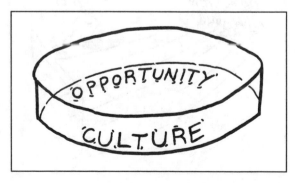

Creating an Op-culture

116

include non-success
- Awareness that non-success must and can be built on
- Autonomy of innovations and NBVs
- Top-level management support and protection for ideas
- Faith in and absolute trust of top management
- Faith and trust of staff by top management
- Positive responses to the provision of all ideas
- A system of educating/training staff in Op-Skills
- A positive expectancy for the generation of ideas
- Open communication

Communication

Several of the key points under other headings ought to be communicated to all your staff, company-wide. Listed below are some of the more important points to communicate.

Staff

Create listening time for upward communication from junior staff. The benefits of listening are incalculable. The costs of not listening are very, very measurable. A few examples will illustrate. IBM failed to listen to one of their top salesmen, Ross Perot, when he suggested that IBM should set up a software design, installa-

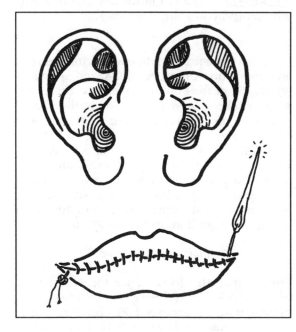

Upward communication

tion, support division, providing service on a fixed contract basis. They pooh-poohed him; he left, set up EDS, and a few years later sold the company for $2.5 billion. Stephen Wozniak approached his employers, Hewlett-Packard, with the microprocessor development that he and his partner had come up with. They turned him down. Wozniak and Jobs promptly set up Apple. Nice one, IBM. Nice one, Hewlett-Packard. Alas, they are not alone; and the list could go on and on. Since neither you nor I want to appear on that list, we'll be listening to our staff, right?

Competitors

Create time to listen to your competitors. As above, failure to do so is very measurable. Hertz thought the new Avis Car Rental at airports was bound to fail, and dismissed any further thought on the matter. That arrogance gave Avis a 3-year clear lead to capture a huge market share, before Hertz acted. Too late. Castlemain's board (Australia's biggest brewery) looked on with condescending amusement as a 'small fry', Alan Bond, tried to buy them out. By the time they realized it was for real, the battle was part of commercial history. So were they. Would you want someone on your board who had proven their judgement of a competitor's actions was less than accurate?

Partners

Business partners, too, fail to listen to each other. Five of Henry Ford's original partners were so appalled by his plan to bring cars within the reach of 'the little people' that they wanted out. Ford bought their stock, and the rest needs no telling.

Op-Spotters are your future

Let it be known that Op-Spotters are where the future is at. And those engaging in this behaviour or supporting those that do can expect to be rewarded.

EXERCISE: What kind of rewards could you offer for support?

Spot opportunities or omit survival

Spread the view that companies don't survive unless they innovate, and that they don't become Opportunity Spotters overnight.

A process of gradual cultural change must take place over a period that is proportional to a

Op-Spotters are the future

company's size. What is each member of staff doing towards it?

Spread the view: innovate or . . .

EXERCISE: How can you spread this view?

Cross-fertilization

Encourage Opportunity-Spotting interaction between departments at all levels. Are departments having TQM type meetings for Op-Spotting? Are the agendas of departmental meetings, and all reports, including an Op-Spotting slot?

EXERCISE: Devise a structure or system to facilitate upward Opportunity-Spotting communication; competitor information communication; inter-departmental opportunity communication; and opportunity communication between the highest officers of the company.

Encourage the notion that all needs of the organization should be served, not just profitability, for example need for innovation, Opportunity Spotting, replacing the old with the new, NBVs.

EXERCISE: How can you convince shareholders (not known for their 'long-termism') and other stakeholders that Op-Spotting and NBV development is a good investment?

Time-scale and innovation realities

Let it be known throughout the company that innovation and opportunity following is characterized by chaos, stops, starts, false stops and false starts.

EXERCISE: Why is innovation like that and why should you warn your staff?

Let it be known that while small innovations and opportunities can be capitalized on quickly, usually at the point of discovery, the larger projects take at least 4 years before they begin to show signs of being successful, let alone any sign of return. This can be seen as a 'J-curve effect'. It is called the 'J-curve effect' because, like the curve of the letter J, there is an immediate and prolonged down-turn and quite a long uphill struggle before you even reach the level you were at before you started. But if you can get through that, things really take off.

Commit to your idea people

Ensure that the idea generator (person) is involved ASAP and throughout the idea development if the idea is to be taken further. Giving an individual an awareness that their ideas could lead to greater things will increase the motivation of all your staff.

EXERCISE: How can you convey to and convince all potential Op-Spotters that they will be invited to be involved in the development of their idea (no matter how lowly the person's position)?

Opportunity-gathering methods

There are several methods available to gather opportunity ideas that your staff generate. Using all of them would be ideal, but not practical. Choose which you prefer; those will work best for you. Others in your company may prefer alternatives. A free choice of methods should be offered. Perhaps the best possible gathering option is to set up an overall scheme but encourage individual managers and supervisors to implement localized schemes of their own choosing (or if they are good leaders, of their staff's choosing).

Contract creativity

In the same way that you would issue invitations for subcontractors to submit a tender for a job, issue an invite for employees and managers to submit a proposal for a particular opportunity area (an area that you want to find opportunities in, but for which you haven't any specific ideas yet). Alternatively, issue an invitation to tender for one of a set number of opportunity contracts. Various groups of employees and managers would then submit their proposals for opportunity ideas they wish to pursue. You then issue 'contracts' and funding to the most promising ideas.

Opportunity review

Conduct a company-wide opportunity review. Each manager is required to submit an opportunity report about her/his section, department or division. Individual members of staff are also invited to submit their own ideas independently. The report should contain a check list of every responsibility a manager has and what opportunities s/he sees in each of those areas.

Opportunity page in every report

Require that each regular report submitted has the first page as an opportunity review.

Require a SWOT analysis (Strengths, Weaknesses, Opportunities, Threats) by com-

Opportunity review

pany, by department (their own and any other they have an interest in), by self. Get these analyses down on paper. No judgement at this stage. Take them to an appointed Op-team/Op-manager for further development then evaluation.

EXERCISE: Prepare a format of what should be included in this opportunity review page.

Suggestion box systems

Many companies already have such a system. Usually it is under-utilized or even actively distrusted by the staff. The box is widely seen as management paying lip-service to the notion of employee participation. If you do have such a system give it a boost, give it some publicity; notify people that you want their ideas, that you will take them seriously, and that you will reward them handsomely and proportionally. Let people see their ideas as a route to promotion and life enhancement. Run the publicity regularly, give staff feedback on how the company and the people who generated the ideas have benefited. Run an opportunity newsletter. Have a box in every department.

EXERCISE: A whole book could be written on how to successfully use a suggestion box scheme. Think up ten more ways you could make your suggestion box scheme more effective and positively regarded by the staff.

Direct approach to Opportunity manager

Appoint an Opportunity manager, a person whose role is to set up opportunity-gathering systems and methods, to educate employees about the benefits of spotting opportunities, who should make themselves known to and trusted by the staff, and who will regularly ask everyone (where possible) in the company for ideas.

EXERCISE: Write the job description for the Opportunity manager. Even if you can't appoint someone, this exercise is worthwhile because your thinking on what is required will be clarified by the exercise.

Opportunity team/task force

Setting up, in one way or another an Opportunity team to find ideas, and take them through to market conception is a seriously strong option. It is a much more controllable and commercially conventional way of doing things. It is likely to gain widespread and ready acceptance. IBM set up such a team to catch up with Apple and develop its own PCs (after having dismissed the PC market – see Unexpected success). Various other large companies use Opportunity teams. There is a tendency to use teams after the idea has been generated.

Opportunity -generating workshop

The GE workout mentioned earlier is a good model for a creativity workshop, with a few alterations. First, the staff and not the CEO (or any other senior manager) should set the agenda for the meeting. Second, there should be no pressure on one person to make an evaluation decision off the top of his/her head in less than 30 seconds. (Remember the 'abominable no man' and his motivations for saying No?) And thirdly, the workshop should be an open forum – anyone who wishes to attend and contribute ideas is to be encouraged. Display a series of public notices so everyone is informed of the meeting.

Opportunity notebook system

Issue all managers, and anyone else who wishes to participate, with an Opportunity Notebook and ask them to enter one opportunity per page, per day, over the period of a month. At the end of the month, gather the books, compile a list of the opportunities and assess them by whichever means you've chosen to adopt. This could be a less pressurized and more spontaneous way of conducting an opportunity review.

Opportunity room

Set aside one room in the organization (or per site) where everyone knows opportunity ideas are gathered. Perhaps have a series of white- or blackboards around the walls of the room. Staff can come in and look at ideas and add to them. Have staff put a signed written copy of their contributions in a secure box so no stroke of brilliance is accidentally erased and lost for ever. And to ensure the idea's originator gets the credit and can be involved if the idea is taken further.

Opportunity competition

Set up a public or internal competition to generate opportunity ideas. The prizes had better be good; if you do this badly it will create an enormous amount of ill will and cynicism. The prizes should include a substantial amount of cash, a percentage of the profits, the job of implementing (or at least being strongly involved in implementing) the idea. The publicity had better include a legally binding guarantee that, if you use any idea submitted that doesn't win a prize, a fixed fee will be paid, and that understanding that agreement is a condition of entry. Failure to include this will put people off entering for fear that 'They'll take my ideas and give the prize to somebody else with an even better idea'. Failure to include the conditions could leave you open to being sued for a very large amount should you use an idea submitted. Consult a lawyer before using this technique.

R&D departments

The conventional way to plan for product succession is to set up a research and development department. Smaller companies can't afford to do so. But they can afford to have part-time R&D personnel, people whose job it is to gather opportunities as they go about their normal work. Opportunity-Spotting is not just about product succession. The part-time R&D personnel can have a wide-ranging brief to research and develop any opportunity.

EXERCISE: Rank the opportunity-gathering methods in order of those you think are most effective. Rank them in order of those most likely to be accepted enthusiastically in your company.

Key roles

Many of the key roles in the process of developing an opportunity have been, or will be, covered elsewhere. The two most important roles are covered below. Generally speaking in every job you should encourage these two.

Role flexibility

Encourage and allow maximum flexibility in roles and job descriptions. Communicate that encouragement by writing it into all job descriptions. Include a section that makes it clear that all staff are expected to contribute to

An idea is championed of . . .

EXERCISE: Why not a committee?

CEO's bypass

For those following through on an opportunity, it is important that staff disapproving of an idea who are in a higher position in the company cannot bully or intimidate the idea champion, or thwart the idea in any way.

To that end, allow and even encourage opportunity-development champions to work outside the normal chain of command and to bypass normal procedures. Issue a 'CEO Bypass Statement' if required.

Flexibility in roles

the process of ongoing improvement, and are expected to actively seek opportunities of an appropriate kind.

EXERCISE: In what other ways could you encourage flexibility in roles?

Champions

Encourage the emergence of Opportunity champions. A champion is a person who is dedicated to the idea and all its potential benefits. Champions are a necessity; either an idea finds a champion or it dies. A champion is one person NOT, absolutely not, a committee.

Chain-of-command bypass

EXERCISE: What other ways of bypassing bureaucracy and destructive bureaucrats can you come up with?

EXERCISE: How will you encourage the practice of your other methods?

Mentors

Search for mentors, sponsors or coaches to protect the champions and fight for innovative projects. Mentors should be very senior people, group board directors in large companies. Ideally they are skilled commercial politicians who are good at circumventing barriers. The barriers are most likely to be found in the middle management ranks, but can exist in any position amongst those who have reached their level of incompetence (Peter Principle).

Encourage mentors

EXERCISE: If not already known to you, how will you identify the mentors, the people who will protect the opportunity idea from all its potential assassins? How can you encourage and motivate the mentors?

Recruiting

Who should you recruit to develop opportunity ideas (assuming it is not going to be exclusive to the person who generated the idea)? And what level of motivation should you expect? Some background information on the kinds of people who get the kind of results you need will help answer these recruitment questions.

We know that communism destroys its best people; it murders wealth-creators, suppresses potential for achievement, stifles innovation and otherwise strangles all that is best in the human spirit. All in the name of equality. Or at least it tries to. Even under such conditions, faced with a certain death sentence if caught, several hundred entrepreneurs functioned and flourished in the old USSR. People like Yan Rokotov and Otar Lazeishvili had such a need for commercial challenge and achievement that they managed to side-step and avoid barriers put up by bureaucrats, bureaucrats the likes of which we can hardly imagine and, hopefully, will never experience. Both these men made substantial financial and social contributions to their country. They were both rewarded with a firing squad (as were many hundred others).

They knew the risks and were willing to take them. That is the kind of motivation you can have in your staff, if you create the right circumstances. If you have a Rokotov or a Lazeishvili in your company, you had better harness their potential quickly or they'll be off doing it for themselves.

How do you identify such talent?

They are usually what others would regard as 'problem people'. These highly charged

122

Opportunity-Spotters may have some attitudes that will not go down well in a large-company culture. They can be awkward, anti-social, and even downright disruptive. They are probably your brightest but most difficult staff; they challenge authority and most definitely think for themselves and probably for others as well. Not surprisingly, they are usually easy to identify, which makes it easy to target them for 'self-selecting recruitment'.

The cause of their 'problems'

The above kinds of problems will exist when they have no goal to focus on. If they are focused (you have found a role that challenges and inspires them), you will witness a breathtaking output of work.

If they are already productive managers, you'll have witnessed your champion recruiting great people, inspiring them to great performances and then burning them out. Their subordinates just can't keep up with the workload example being set for them. Probably because of the different approach your champion has to work. Since we can all play for much longer than we can work, you can probably attribute the marathon performances to your champion's ability to see work as play. Although, it is unlikely that s/he has to force themselves to adopt this perception. 'Work', to them, probably, 'is more fun than fun', to quote a comment made by Trammell Crow, the hugely successful Dallas real-estate developer, in 1986.

If you have such a dynamo on your payroll, you ought to allow staff to move on, if they wish, to work with another manager before they are burned out. A manager with a high staff turnover may be one of the opportunity champions every company seeks, or a serious personnel headache, depending on how you handle him/her.

Self-selection

Our motivation is maximal towards those things we choose to do. While many employees function like zombies while at work, as soon as the whistle blows they miraculously turn into highly skilled experts in their chosen hobbies. The point is, they *have to* work to earn a living, but they *choose* to indulge in their personal interests.

Where possible, it is preferable to encourage self-selection of specific Opportunity managers (champions) or on to Opportunity teams.

Self-recruiting

EXERCISE: Why self-selection?

Positive and challenging thinkers

Encourage people who have a positive attitude to risk uncertainty. Individuals with a history of change-making (or at least attempting change) are the most desirable.

EXERCISE: How many can you think of now?

Team or individual

One of the biggest decisions in opportunity developing, is whether to recruit teams or individuals for each of the required tasks at each stage. To aid that decision, here are some thoughts on their relative merits and demerits:

Merits of individual:

1 Ownership and commitment level.
2 Reward and remuneration (personal identification with results).
3 Goal setting – objectives easy to define, explain and monitor with one person.
4 Identification and support – finding such individuals and supporting them is easy.
5 Cost – budget developed rapidly; will be cheap; risk more manageable.
6 Morale, talent and example – support the ethic that individuals can make it;

Team v. individual

keeps good intrapreneurial talent in the company.

7 Know-how + skill-level of individual increases.

Demerits of individual:

1 Range and scope of project – narrower. Limited by strengths, insights and experiences of individual.
2 Relationships – intrapreneurs *can be* volatile people. Many have a self-destructive mechanism and can often alienate those people they need most.
3 Outsider syndrome – intrapreneurs may be seen as 'outsiders' and be sidelined and ignored.
4 Creative links – one person may not see chances for synergy or other profitable connections.
5 Failure – is more difficult to deal with in a single person.
6 Company fit/product credibility fit and so on – the risk of a failure of fit is increased with a small number of contributors.

Team advantages:

1 Range, scope and credibility are higher.
2 Failure – group will be self-supporting.
3 Fit – more chance of fit on all criteria.
4 Support – group self-supporting.
5 Energy levels – equilibrium is established, so a 'downer' doesn't bring the project to a halt.
6 Skill range and collective know-how – bound to be better than in an individual,

provided that sufficiently good communication is available to use the enhanced skills and so on.

Team disadvantages:

1 Ownership – or rather lack of it (shared [ir]responsibility phenomenon).
2 Organizational difficulties (for example, diary clashes and so on).
3 Clarity of focus – poor, unless very tightly monitored.
4 Time and cost greater (to pay for communication costs alone!).
5 Divisive morale effect – 'You're not in the Op-Team'.
6 Team membership mistakes.
7 Opportunity development skills – easier to find or equip one person with requisite skills.

EXERCISE: What other advantages or disadvantages to either team or individuals can you think of?

EXERCISE: Need it be team *or* individual? Are they mutually exclusive? What mid-way options are there between the two extremes of team *v.* individual?

EXERCISE: When would you consider it necessary to use a team and when would you use an individual?

EXERCISE: If you choose a team, who should be on it and what should its remit be?

Who's ON the team?

Obviously the 'who will be on the team' is dependent on what the team will be doing. Different knowledge and skill will be required to achieve differing objectives. However, if you do set up (as opposed to self-recruiting) an opportunity team, recruit people with high commitment as a priority, and absolutely NOT people with high skill and low commitment.

Why?

1 There are so many obstacles in the way of successful innovation that only the most committed will have the strength to push it all the way through.
2 Those with high knowledge or skill and low commitment can be called on at any time (for a short time) in an advisory capacity if required.

EXERCISE: Which famous examples of commitment being the single largest factor in the success of a major innovation can you cite?

Who's OFF the team?

Remove non-attenders/non-contributors/ non-performers and negative influences from opportunity teams ASAP.

Remove negative influences ASAP

EXERCISE: Why? How can you do this and still maintain their commitment to the opportunity culture you are trying to create?

Who's not off the team?

While you need to remove negative influences ASAP, you should try to seek out, encourage and leave the channels open for the presentation of dissident views.

These views are most accurate when coming from normally positive people who can present a well-argued, rational case. Dissident views can show you how to alter an idea in such a way that it will be more successful or avoid complete failure. Failure to listen to dissident views about the booster 'O' rings contributed to the NASA Challenger disaster.

Reward and remuneration

How you reward the intrapreneurs, Opportunity Spotters, champions and mentors in your company will be perhaps the most unusual remuneration system you'll ever oversee.

Intrapreneurs, like entrepreneurs, are not interested in promotion in the conventional sense of the word, neither are they interested in empire building – they are, as we have seen, motivated by challenge. They seek varied and multi-skilled roles. Entrepreneurs, like intrapreneurs, seek the passion and independence that a start-up, development or recovery situation gives them. They are less interested in consuming and more in consummating their ideas. As can be seen by looking at any cross-section of entrepreneurs, the results that one person can achieve with this passion are simply breathtaking.

You can go some way towards harnessing this power in your company if you offer appropriate reward and remuneration.

Bell Atlantic do so with what they call their Champion Programme. Any employee who has a good idea is able to leave their job for a while on full pay etc., is trained in the various relevant skills (business planning, project management . . .), is given a budget to invest in the project, is able to invest up to 10 per cent of their salary in exchange for bonuses of up to 5 per cent of revenues if the project makes it to market. The early results are good. With several patents obtained and several more pending. Watch that space!

There are several guiding principles to help you decide what reward structure you should establish.

Ownership

PRINCIPLE: The more ownership the higher the commitment level.

Commitment can be maximized by rewarding champions with:

● Share options
● Profit sharing
● Equity stakes.

Apply this principle even if the persons concerned are going to be moving on to another project after the set up is complete.

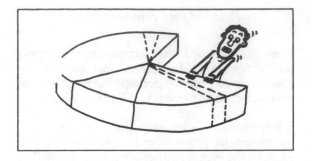

Reward and remuneration

EXERCISE: Which guidelines should you use to decide on the level of each of the above possible rewards?

Chosen rewards

PRINCIPLE: A chosen reward has more motivating power.

Reward with what the Op-Spotter chooses, which might be:

● Recognition
● Time off
● Time freedom to develop ideas
● Venture money.

The latter two of the above will probably pay a high return to the company. And, bearing in mind what was said about consummating

Chosen rewards have . . .

ideas, it is likely that those are the options your champion will want to choose.

Champion-focused rewards

PRINCIPLE: Tailor rewards to suit the individual's choice NOT the company's convenience.

Do so by allowing flexibility of reward with such devices as bonus in lieu of promotion – This applies to the intrapreneur who does not want to head a large department/division, but is operating at that level. Or promotion – to the appropriate level in terms of pay conditions, title, status and so on, but without the departmental responsibilities. Or political clout – the

more influence an Op-Spotter, mentor or champion has within the company, the more likely s/he is to succeed.

EXERCISE: How could you create a situation in which you could give the intrapreneur a choice?

EXERCISE: What would happen to the champion's attitude towards the company if s/he saw peers being promoted for merely managing when s/he was being overlooked for creating new businesses and securing the future of the company?

EXERCISE: How can you give political clout in your organization?

EXERCISE: Decide on the criteria for giving the rewards.

EXERCISE: In what way should rewards vary from idea to idea (opportunity project to project)?

Ongoing innovation 'pass mark'

Reward managers on the basis of 1 in 20 suc-

Reward managers

cess rate. In other words, if 5 per cent of their ongoing innovative attempts succeed, rewards should be forthcoming. Any better than that ratio should result in higher or more rewards.

EXERCISE: What kind of rewards should you offer for what kinds of innovative attempts? (Note the principles above.) Should you categorize different areas of innovation so that everyone in the company feels they can help? The areas for Op-Spotting could be cost savings, sales increases, NBVs . . .

EXERCISE: Compile a list of other areas for Op-Spotting.

Prizes and publicity

If the person is willing, make a public figure of anyone doing better than 1/20. Award annual prizes for the three best innovations, ideas, improvements or however many you think is necessary to achieve the motivational effect you desire. Try to ensure that prizes go to those who really deserve them rather than to those whose only skill is in obtaining credit for the efforts of others.

EXERCISE: What criteria would you use to award prizes so all can see the process is fair?

So it didn't work out

PRINCIPLE: Reward for Op-Spotting activi-

ties that didn't go to plan.

Reward those Op-Spotting activities that didn't go to plan but which still made a contribution of some kind (if only to put to rest an idea that everyone thought might work).

The 19/20 not-to-plans should not be regarded as, perceived as, or presented as failures.

EXERCISE: How can you reward not-to-plan results and with what? Set up a structure.

EXERCISE: How should you present 'not-to-plans' so as to encourage everyone to continue trying?

Minimize risk to individuals

Seek to minimize the risk to individuals for being Op-Spotters, for example, if someone is put in charge of a NBV or other innovation programme and it doesn't go to plan, they should be allowed to return to their previous post . . . with no penalty or tarnish on their career. In fact, there should be merit attached to the fact that they tried, and to the expertise that they no doubt acquired in the course of the project.

EXERCISE: What more can you do to ensure minimal risk to individuals?

Return route option

Setting up a reward system and means of minimizing the risk to an individual is a lot easier than dealing with the morale of a loyal member of staff who has put their heart and soul into a project for goodness knows how long, only to see it dropped, or not go to plan. The following lines are glib and completely fail to deal with the emotional pain associated with such a situation, but the ideas they contain may be the basis for your morale-boosting discussions with the person concerned.

● Having to learn from one's experiences is painful; not learning from them is crippling.
● For every bad choice, there is at least one reason to rejoice. Good judgement comes from experience and experience comes from bad judgement.
● Experience is what you get when you didn't get what you wanted, unless of course, what you wanted was to learn from your experience.

Ask your 'nearly made it' champion questions like: What did we learn from this? Tell me five things we learned from this? What skill did you develop and improve on the project? In short, ask questions that require your champion to focus on the positive to be answered.

PRINCIPLE: Encourage with incentives not sanctions.

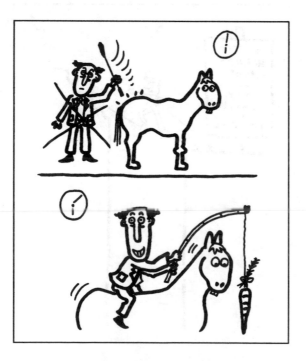

Incentives v. penalties

But if you must have sanctions, make them the withholding of rewards. We know that penalties, with a few exceptions, don't work as well as factors related to reward provision in attempts to alter behaviour.

The withholding of rewards from poor performers tends to focus their minds on changing their behaviour to obtain the available rewards. At the very least, they will try to convince you that a change has taken place, which in itself makes them more persuadable by you.

Training and managing the managers

How do you train staff and managers to be entrepreneurial, to be internal risk takers, to be Opportunity Spotters? By communicating the needs for, and benefits of, Opportunity Spotting. By teaching them some of the methods used to spot, seek and create opportunities . . . (*Is this sounding familiar?*) By showing them how to enhance ideas. By giving them methods to evaluate ideas. (*It should be.*) By alerting them to the barriers they are likely to encounter and to some methods for overcoming them. (*Yes, that's right; teach them the same elements that appear here.*) And finally convey the elements that go into developing an opportunity and opportunity culture.

To achieve all of the above, you may have to teach a few old dogs a few new tricks. You may have to actively encourage your top executives to take risks and get involved in the Op-Spotting process. Many of your senior managers, perhaps including the CEO, will have climbed the corporate ladder the conventional way. They may be highly skilled political operators, but lacking in entrepreneurial skills. There is no doubt such people will be able to master the new skills quickly and completely. They will, however, be tempted to oversee and direct the process, thereby denying the company access to the wealth of ideas that could come from their own massive storehouse of commercial knowledge. Encourage them to contribute personally; they'll probably enjoy the fun aspects of many of the Opportunity Spotting methods.

EXERCISE: How can you encourage them?

Keep the NBVs close

Given the political skills mentioned above, you probably won't have to encourage top executives to maintain close contact with NBVs and

Execs close to NBVs

its/their potential customers.

EXERCISE: But , if you do have to, how will you do so?

Training philosophies

As part of your opportunity-culture development programme introduce the following training philosophies.

- Staff should acquire whatever new skills the company needs, particularly for finding and developing opportunities.
- The company will provide all the training resources and the necessary support to those acquiring the desired skills. If that is not possible, the next point should apply.
- The company will pay more to those who have acquired the necessary skills.
- Staff should, on an ongoing basis, develop themselves towards their next logical promotion, or their next preferred transfer; towards contributing to the process of ongoing improvement in the company; and towards being able to actively seek opportunities.

EXERCISE: What other training practices or philosophies would help? How will you communicate the new policies?

Development by involvement

You should ensure that the idea generator (person) is involved ASAP and throughout the idea development, if the idea is to be taken

further.

EXERCISE: How can you convey to and convince all potential Op-Spotters that they will be invited to be involved in the development of their idea (no matter how lowly the person's position)?

Develop your budding spotters, champions and mentors wherever possible. If someone comes up with an idea, and either the idea is

Develop Op-Spotters

not suitable or they lack the skills to take the lead in developing it, then give them a chance to play an important part in that or some other project. Or as was mentioned previously, to develop the necessary skills themselves.

EXERCISE: What other ways could you develop Op-Spotters?

Naughty, naughty!

Penalize (or rather withhold rewards from) managers who don't invest in innovation, Op-Spotting and improvement seeking. And from those who make cuts that will cost more in the long run.

129

EXERCISE: Should this be publicly stated? If so how?

Ensure such managers stay in post long

Consequences of under-investment

enough (withhold promotion) to experience personally the consequences of their under-investment.

EXERCISE: Why? Should that policy be publicly stated?

This is another policy you won't ever have to carry out. As soon as such people realize what is expected, they start changing their ways.

Planning/policies/administration

Administration

Have a minimal requirement for administration and reporting from your Op-Team or champion. Too much and you will thwart the dynamic spontaneity of their creativity. Entrepreneurs and intrapreneurs usually hate doing administration, but recognize the need for it. Allocate administrative support so your champions are not demotivated by doing something they hate.

EXERCISE: What admin./reporting will you require? Are you sure that won't be too much?

Planning

Opportunity development requires extremely

Planning and reporting

flexible planning. Different planning methods will be most productive at the various development stages.

Early stage planning

Normal planning procedures will not, and cannot, work in the early stages of an idea's development, because of the stop–start, progress–chaos nature that is inherent in all creative processes. Planning 'on the hoof' is the most intelligent response to dealing with unforeseen and unforeseeable problems and barriers.

Parallel planning

If you do feel a need to plan in advance, devise several alternative or parallel plans to achieve the same goal. However, take note that parallel planning may reduce the commitment to follow any one route to completion. Faced with a serious obstacle, the smartest action may be to take another route. Don't allow 'Let's try another route' to substitute for dogged persistence.

EXERCISE: How can you judge, when someone is opting for another route, that they are not showing the first signs of lack of commitment or of giving up?

Conventional business planning

Business plan as late as possible in the evolution of an idea and only when the idea is sufficiently developed to stand it.

130

When the idea is ready to have its implementation plan drawn up, do it all in one go. Don't plan it in stages as you go along. At every stage, a large number of people will want to put their mark on it, leading to all sorts of delays and interruptions. The Japanese are aware of that probability, and consequently spend more time (40 per cent in Japan v. 25 per cent in USA) in planning and consensus gaining, and then stick to the decisions. They have a third of the problems after launch that USA companies have.

EXERCISE: What criteria will you use to decide when the idea is ready to enter the formal business planning stage?

Separate entity

For a seriously good innovation, an NBV (New Business Venture) should be set up and allowed to exist as a separate unit. Allow it to evolve its own structures; don't impose parental company structures on it.

EXERCISE: Why? Who should decide on the structure?

Opportunity development schedule

An Opportunity Spotted need not culminate in a big new business. Indeed most Ops will be minor improvements by very small innovative jumps, made by quite ordinary people with quite extraordinarily positive attitudes and pride in performance.

If you have set up the right culture and reward system, the smaller opportunities and

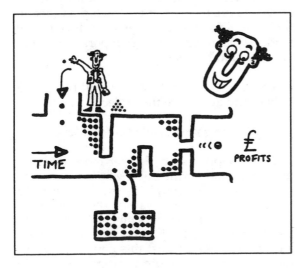

Opportunity pipeline

improvements will flow constantly. The flow of larger ideas will need more attention. Use the various opportunity-gathering methods to ensure you have sufficient numbers of projects in development. Initiate opportunity developments with appropriately staggered lead times so you have sufficient coming through to cope with the 5 per cent success rate.

EXERCISE: How many is sufficient?

An example of the time-scale involved might help you answer. It took Gideon Sundback, the inventor of the modern day 'zip', 14 years from the point of conception to obtain any worthwhile return. Drug manufacturing companies will tell you lead times are thought to be good if they come in at less than a decade.

EXERCISE: What other ways can you use to keep your opportunity pipeline flowing?

Hooked on biggles

Avoid the temptation to depend on 'the big one', a great idea that looks as though it has great potential. Keep other ideas coming as well. You don't want to be in the position in which Clive Sinclair found himself when his 'big one', the C5, became a 'not to plan'.

Goal setting

Encourage staff to focus on opportunities by setting goals for each employee, manager, department, division, director and so on to generate innovations, improvements, and opportunities on a weekly, monthly or quarterly basis. 3M require each division to generate 25 per cent of sales from new products.

Target specific people for particular types of opportunity. For instance, sales managers will be best equipped to find opportunities in sales methods, add on products . . . Bureaucrats are most suited to finding opportunities in information and administration systems.

Allow staff time and freedom to explore opportunity ideas. You may want to go even further and allocate a certain percentage of the working week to Opportunity Spotting.

EXERCISE: In what other ways could you encourage staff to focus on opportunity hunting?

EXERCISE: How will you guide staff to balance the Op-Spotting requirements with their other responsibilities?

When you are setting targets, make sure they are challenging and inspiring.

EXERCISE: At the risk of asking the obvious, why?

Avoid setting purely numerical goals – they are less inspiring than qualitative achievement goals. (This will go against the grain of some people hearing it, but most entrepreneurs would not be even slightly surprised!)

EXERCISE: What kind of goals should be set?

All too often NBVs go wrong because clearly defined goals are not set and universally understood. Ensure that the people on the NBV know the objectives for the project, that they understand them and believe them to be worthwhile.

Financial issues

Conventional financial analysis will produce some very strange effects on both your planning and on your champions. Avoid conventional financial analysis of opportunity ideas and NBVs. Or at least avoid drawing any serious conclusions from F/A. As discussed previously there are no ways of measuring the hidden resources contained in opportunity ideas. If the struggling young Walt Disney had

Financial issues

subjected his early cartoon character ideas to strict financial analysis and made his decision on those bases, do you think we would have the wealth of entertainment he created, available to us today?

EXERCISE: Why should you avoid conventional financial analysis? And what means of measuring the potential in an innovation or opportunity idea should you use? (If you can answer the last question, publish it, quickly; you'll make a fortune. Professors of Strategy, Accounting, Economics and Finance have struggled with that one for quite some time.)

Assassination avoidance

In the early stages of an idea's development, keep costs down to minimize exposure; political assassinations of the brilliant, and of brilliant

ideas, are common. We have already explained the motives for rubbishing or destroying an idea. It is often smartest to develop an idea to the point where it is either clear that it will work, or that it has so much support that to rubbish it would be career suicide.

EXERCISE: At what point should you 'go public' and announce the project?

Trusting people more than numbers

Trust the Opportunity Spotter more than the numbers. Good bank managers and venture capitalists do, but why? Vision, character and commitment have no way of showing themselves on any financial document. It may be an unsatisfactory and subjective basis for making a decision to say 'I trust this person with this idea', but it is no more subjective than any numbers you would put down on what would

132

be no more than a wish list passing itself off as a business plan.

Intellectual capital

As an idea is being developed, encourage and ensure maximum use of intellectual and effort capital is made before hard cash is used.

Use intellectual capital

Access to response

Sideways loading

Sideways load the NBV costs, in the same way that a growing foetus does. You would not expect a foetus to be self-supporting from conception. Neither is an NBV.

It takes time and money to complete the commercial gestation period successfully. And like a new-born baby, an NBV requires support for

Human nature is such that most people see throwing money at a problem as the best solution, or the best way to obtain a solution. It may well be if you are solving problems others have already solved. But when you are breaking new ground, money will not be sufficient.

EXERCISE: What criteria will you use to decide that intellectual and effort capital have been maximally used before releasing funds?

Multi-sourced budget

However when the time comes, allow the team or champion access to several financial and other necessary resources to spread the load between departments.

EXERCISE: Which financial sources are appropriate in your company, and what kind of access should the champion/team have?

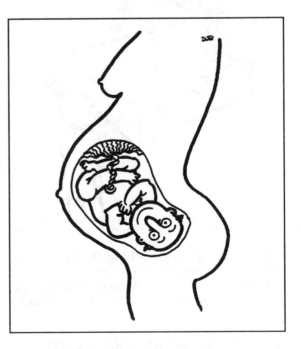

Sideways loading

quite some time after birth, although, hopefully, not quite as long!

EXERCISE: What would happen if you didn't sideways load?

Commercial tithing

When you do your next round of budget planning, allocate a proportion of the budget for Opportunity-Spotting activities. Each manager should be expected to invest a percentage of his/her budget in seeking and developing opportunities, innovations and improvements for the future.

EXERCISE: What would happen if you didn't?

Measuring your Op-Spot performance

Performance in any field can only be improved if it is recorded, monitored, evaluated and modified. Corporate innovation and Opportunity Spotting are no exceptions.

Ideally, the monitoring of your innovative performance should be conducted by someone other than, and not associated with, the person

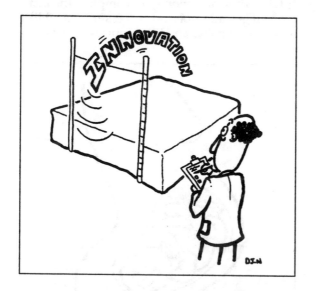

who is charged with setting the system up. And the administrative responsibilities for monitoring the system should under no circumstances be placed on your opportunity champions.

It will be down to each company to devise its own monitoring system. Here are some guide-

line questions:

- How many training sessions have been organized?
- Lasting how long?
- Covering what material?
- How many staff have been trained?
- How many trainers have been trained?
- How many managers/directors have been trained?
- How many managers are participants in opportunity exercises?
- How many senior managers have been opportunity mentors?
- How many opportunity publicizing notices have been issued?
- What percentage of senior managers have been formally involved in spreading the opportunity-culture message?
- How many opportunity teams are functioning?
- What percentage of employees are involved in them?
- What has prevented those who have not participated?
- How many proposals is each department/section generating?
- How many of these are realistic sensible ideas?
- Which gathering method produces the largest number of ideas?
- Which method produces the highest percentage of successfully implemented ideas?
- What percentage of ideas is dropped at the evaluation stage?
- How many ideas are successfully implemented?
- How well-completed are the opportunity reviews?
- What response rates do the opportunity-gathering methods give?
- How many patent applications have been generated?
- How many new products have been created?
- What percentage of revenues is going into R&D?
- What market reaction have new products had?

The list could go on . . .

EXERCISE: What other factors should you measure?

More examples of successful opportunity cultures

Japan used to be a 'creative imitation' or 'me too' culture, but now they are world-class innovators with companies like Canon, Toshiba, Hitachi, Sony . . . Canon in particular has an impressive record. It adds 800 to 900 patents a year to its already enormous list. Their history of innovation has created a long-term revolution in the company's fortunes from systematic day-to-day evolution. In the 1950s, they were a camera company; in the 1960s they were applying optics to the office environment; in the 1970s they were applying laser technology to the office; in the 1980s they pioneered the bubble jet; in the 1990s the possibilities include applications of opto-electronics, more sophisticated electron beam applications and . . .? The strategy they use is to seek, spot or create opportunities which are close to their core competences.

Sony has an impressive record too: they produce four new products a day; they have been responsible for the Walkman, CDs (with Philips), VCRs (Betamax), and Nintendo Games. Sony spends 5.7 per cent of its revenues of $26 billion on R&D. They have an interesting recruitment policy, preferring to hire optimistic, open-minded people with a wide range of interests – for all roles. Sony also has an unusual promotion policy – self-promotion. Staff are permitted and encouraged to seek out new positions in the company and are able to move to them freely if successful.

In America, Polaroid Corporation create interdisciplinary teams to work on projects. Nothing unusual in that but they also pay their employees for acquiring new skills the company needs (even if the up-skilling is not associated with a promotion). The Polaroid approach led to the development of Helios, their innovative medical imaging system being developed from scratch to production in just 3 years!

3M have a perpetual innovation policy. Each division is required to generate at least 25 per cent of its sales from products that didn't exist 5 years ago. Does it work? 3M's list of 50 000 new products seems to suggest so.

EXERCISE: Devise all the materials, memos, notices, announcements, etc. you need to start the culture change.

EXERCISE: Take the ideas that came through the evaluation process and apply the principles in the section just covered. How did the way you planned to implement the idea(s) change as compared to the way you envisaged implementing them prior to assimilating this section?

FINAL EXERCISE: Devise an Opportunity-Spotting culture and strategies to suit you, the company, your position in the company and the market within which it operates.

8

Conclusion

The need to plan for product evolution and succession was clear to you before you bought this book. A brief analysis of the needs and benefits at the outset probably reinforced your thinking or, at the very least, gave you some material with which to convince your company peers why they should listen to your views on corporate creativity.

An awareness of the material presented should enable you to spot opportunities, to know where to seek them, and to know what needs to be done when you observe a situation in which an ingredient is missing from a known opportunity recipe.

You will be able to explain to one and all that the idea is the starting point, the raw material that forms the basis of survival and growth.

From that base point, you can enhance and build on initial ideas which you, your staff, or opportunity team have generated. You can take ideas to the point where they are worthy of consideration. You will be able to demonstrate that ideas must be enhanced and fine-tuned to take them from concept to serious proposal.

In addition to your normal decision-making tools, you now have several methods of evaluating opportunity ideas, methods that take account of the difficulty in attempting to quantify the future value of adult opportunities when they are still in nappies, or perhaps only just conceived.

You are now able to identify, anticipate and deal with several different species of opportunity-eating, predatory barriers. With a bit of effort you can now banish the barriers to starvation in corporate Siberia.

The home, nursery and school environment in which you bring up your opportunity children will determine whether they will be well-adjusted contributors to your corporate purse if, or when, they reach maturity.

In your attempts to be a good parent you will harness several other powerful forces; the power of the shared strategic vision, the group cohesion of a joint mission, and the dynamism of empowering those most likely to know how to obtain results.

When you put this book down, make that act not your finishing point, but your starting point. Grow beyond this material. Put your newly acquired intellectual skills into practice, fine-tune them, schedule follow-up sessions in your diary, plan training sessions for yourself and your staff.

Finally, the era has come where capital and physical resources are secondary in power and value to intellectual resources (IR). As information technology becomes progressively more powerful and widespread, IR will increase its superiority. Corporate creativity allows you to tap into, and harness the IR you already have on your payroll. Your company is going to survive and grow in a world where intellectual resources are king, if you use the power contained in *Opportunity Spotting*.

References and bibliography

Ansoff, I. (1987),*Corporate Strategy*, London: Penguin.

Barranger, J. (1991), *Knowing When To Quit*, Wellingborough: Thorsons.

Birmingham Technology Transfer (1987), *Proceedings Of The 1987 Symposium On Innovation and Entrepreneurship*, Birmingham, UK.

Burns, P. and Kippenberger, T. (1988), *Entrepreneur*, London: Macmillan Press.

Casson, M. (1982), *The Entrepreneur*, Oxford: Martin Robertson.

Churchill, N. C. and Lewis, V. L. (1983) 'The Five Stages Of Small Business Growth', *Harvard Business Review*, May–June, 30–50.

Davis, W. (1987), *The Innovators*, London: Ebury Press.

De Bono, E. (1978), *Opportunities*, London: Pelican Books.

De Bruicker, F. S. and Summe, G. L. (1985), 'Make Sure Your Customers Keep Coming Back', *Harvard Business Review*, Jan–Feb, 92–8.

Dowie, J. and Lefrere, P. (eds) (1980), *Risk and Chance*, Milton Keynes: Open University Press.

Drucker, P. F. (1985), *Innovation and Entrepreneurship*, London: Heinemann.

Economist Intelligence Unit (1987), *Intrapreneurship In Action*, Economist Publications Ltd.

Firnstahl, T. W. (1986), 'Letting Go', *Harvard Business Review*, Sept–Oct, 14–17.

Foster, T. R. V. (1991), *101 Ways To Generate Great Ideas*, London: Kogan Page.

Gilder, G. (1984), *The Spirit Of Enterprise*, Middlesex, UK: Viking.

Gelatt, H. B. (1991), *Creative Decision Making*, London: Kogan Page.

Hawken, P. (1989), *Growing A Business*, London: Methuen.

Kets De Vries, M. F. R. (1977), 'The Entrepreneurial Personality: A Person At The Crossroads', *The Journal Of Management Studies*, Feb, 35–57.

Kets De Vries, M. F. R. (1985), 'The Dark Side Of Entrepreneurship', *Harvard Business Review*, Nov–Dec, 160–7.

Kindler, H. S. (1990), *Risk Taking*, London: Kogan Page.

Lessem, R. (1983), 'The Art Of Entrepreneurship', *Journal Of General Management*, 8(3), 39–49.

Modiano, P. and Ni-Chionna, O. (1986), 'Breaking Into The Big Time', *Management Today*, November, 82–4.

Nolan, V. (1989), *The Innovators Handbook*, London: Spere Books Ltd.

Pinchot, G. (1985), *Intrapreneurship*, New York: Harper & Row.

Porter, M. E. (1980), *Competitive Strategy*, Free Press, USA.

Poulet, R. (1986), 'How Businesses Bust Themselves', *Management Today*, July, 68–71.

Reichard, C. J. (1985), 'Industrial Selling: Beyond Price and Persistance', *Harvard Business Review*, March–April, 127–33.

Robinson, D. F. (1990), *The Naked Entrepreneur*, London: Kogan Page.

Robinson, J. (1985), *Risk Takers*, London: George Allen & Unwin.

Robinson, J. (1990), *The Risk Takers Five Years On*, London: Mandarin.

Rusk, T. and N. (1988), *Mind Traps*, Wellingborough: Thorsons.

Slater, S. (1987), *Corporate Recovery*, London: Penguin.

Stevenson, H. H. and Gumpert, D. E. (1985), 'The Heart Of Entrepreneurship', *Harvard Business Review*, March–April, 85–94.

Van Grundy, A. B. (1992), *Idea Power*, American Management Association, USA.

Vernon, P. E. (ed.) (1976), *Creativity*, London: Penguin.

Index

INDEX